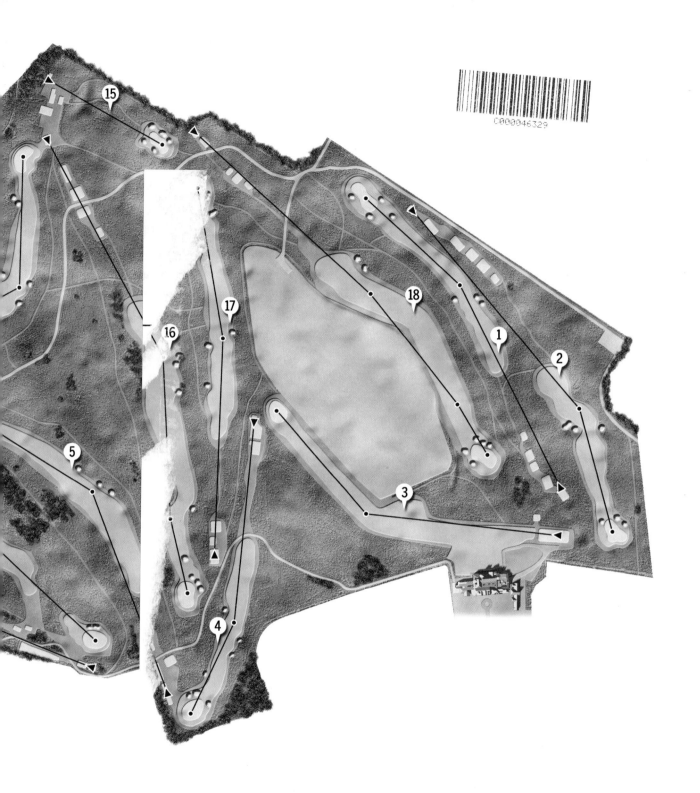

Based in St Andrews, The R&A organises
The Open Championship, major amateur
events and international matches. Together
with the United States Golf Association, The
R&A governs the game worldwide, jointly
administering the Rules of Golf, Rules of
Amateur Status, Equipment Standards and
World Amateur Golf Rankings. The R&A's
working jurisdiction is global, excluding
the United States and Mexico.

The R&A is committed to working for golf
and supports the growth of the game
internationally and the development and
management of sustainable golf facilities.
The R&A operates with the consent of 152
organisations from the amateur and
professional game and on behalf of over 30
million golfers in 138 countries.

RandA.org

Aurum Press
74-77 White Lion Street, London N1 9PF

Published 2014 by Aurum Press

Copyright © 2014 R&A Championships Limited

Course illustration by Graham Gaches

Project coordinator: Sarah Wooldridge
Additional thanks to NTT Data and Strokesaver.

A CIP catalogue record for this book is available
from the British Library

ISBN-13: 978 1 78131 442 5

Designed and produced by Davis Design
Colour retouching by Luciano Retouching Services, Inc.
Printed in Slovenia by Svet Print d.o.o.

EDITOR
Andy Farrell

WRITERS AND PHOTOGRAPHERS

Writers	Getty Images	The R&A	Golf Editors
Peter Dixon	Andrew Redington	Ross Kinnaird	Richard Martin-Roberts
Andy Farrell	Tom Pennington	David Cannon	Jaime Lawson
John Hopkins	Stuart Franklin	Warren Little	Scott Halleran
Lewine Mair	Matthew Lewis	Ian Walton	Ker Robertson
Art Spander	Mike Ehrmann	Richard Heathcote	Rob Harborne
Alistair Tait		Mark Runnacles	

Foreword

By Rory McIlroy

This victory at The Open was for my mum. My dad was there when I won my first two Major Championships, but this was the first time I had won in front of my mum. It was great to see her there at the back of the 18th green and to see how much it meant to her — how much it meant to us all.

The support from my parents, and all the sacrifices they made for me while I was growing up, has been incredible. They are always there for me, whether my golf is less than perfect or when it's all come together, like now, in another Major win. That has been great stability for me.

To be introduced as the "Champion Golfer of the Year" and to hold the Claret Jug was an incredible feeling. The Open is the one we all want, the one we strive for. I must thank The R&A for putting on such a great Championship and for everything it does for golf and the development of the game. The R&A is a great organisation and I am glad to be its Champion this year.

The members of Royal Liverpool Golf Club were very hospitable, generous and professional, presenting us with a wonderful golf course to play. It was an excellent test of golf and I was delighted with the way it was set up — and how I was able to take advantage of that.

And the support for all the players from fans who turned up in their thousands and thousands was absolutely fantastic — even for a Manchester United fan like me!

While I will always savour what I achieved this week at Hoylake, there are also some exciting times ahead. I look forward to trying to complete the career Grand Slam at the Masters in April and I can't wait to defend the Claret Jug at one of my favourite Open venues, St Andrews, next year.

The Championship Committee

CHAIRMAN
Peter Unsworth

DEPUTY CHAIRMAN
Paul Baxter

COMMITTEE

Stuart Allison	Martin Ebert
Andrew Bathurst	Stuart Graham
David Boyle	John Louden
Clive Brown	Charlie Maran
Tony Disley	Andrew Stracey

CHIEF EXECUTIVE
Peter Dawson

EXECUTIVE DIRECTOR – CHAMPIONSHIPS
Johnnie Cole-Hamilton

EXECUTIVE DIRECTOR – RULES AND EQUIPMENT STANDARDS
David Rickman

Introduction

By Peter Unsworth
Chairman of the Championship Committee of The R&A

This year's Open Championship at Royal Liverpool was memorable in a number of ways. The Hoylake links, which was presented in outstanding condition once again, produced a great Champion in Rory McIlroy. The young Northern Irishman led from start to finish but had to fend off challenges from the likes of Sergio Garcia and Rickie Fowler to lift the Claret Jug. In doing so, he became only the third player, after Jack Nicklaus and Tiger Woods, to win their third Major Championship by the age of 25. It was a remarkable performance and I am sure golf fans all over the world will be looking forward to Rory's defence of the Championship at St Andrews next year.

For spectators this was the most connected Open Championship ever. With a free wireless network covering the entire course, spectators in the grandstands and tented village areas were able to access a wide range of digital content, including video highlights and scoring, on their mobile phones and tablet devices. We introduced innovations such as a "this just in" service for users of the Official Open App which gave them updates and video highlights of any significant action from other parts of the course. The App proved extremely popular and helped give users a greatly enhanced experience of watching The Open.

The galleries were wonderful throughout the week. Nowhere was the atmosphere more special than in the grandstand around the 18th green. Surrounding three sides of the green it proved to be a wonderful arena for the players and spectators alike.

I would like to thank the Captain, Championship Committee and all members and staff of Royal Liverpool Golf Club together with the hundreds of volunteers for their enormous contribution towards the success of the 2014 Open Championship.

THE OPEN CHAMPIONSHIP QUALIFYING SERIES

JAPAN

Mizuno Open   **29 May - 1 June**

Dong-Kyu Jang, Korea
Juvic Pagunsan, Philippines
Hyung-Tae Kim, Korea
Tomohiro Kondo, Japan

THAILAND

OQS Thailand			6-7 March
Hiroshi Iwata, Japan	68	71	139
Cheng-tsung Pan*, Taiwan	70	70	140
Ashun Wu, China	72	68	140
Yoshinobu Tsukada[(P)], Japan	72	69	141

AUSTRALIA

Emirates Australian Open   28 Nov - 1 Dec

John Senden, Australia
Rhein Gibson, Australia
Bryden Macpherson, Australia

USA

Quicken Loans National	26-29 June

Shawn Stefani, USA
Charley Hoffman, USA
Ben Martin, USA
Brendan Steele, USA

Greenbrier Classic	3-6 July

George McNeill, USA
Chris Stroud, USA
Cameron Tringale, USA
Billy Hurley III, USA

John Deere Classic	10-13 July

Brian Harman, USA

Royal Liverpool ★

THE OPEN QUALIFYING SERIES EUROPE 2014

EUROPE

Irish Open	19-22 June

Edoardo Molinari, Italy
Danny Willett, England
Matthew Baldwin, England

Alstom Open de France	3-6 July

Robert Karlsson, Sweden
Michael Hoey, Northern Ireland
Victor Riu, France

Aberdeen Asset Management Scottish Open	10-13 July

Kristoffer Broberg, Sweden
Tyrrell Hatton, England
Scott Jamieson, Scotland

FINAL QUALIFYING

Gailes Links		1 July	
Marc Warren, Scotland	69	64	133
Jamie McLeary, Scotland	63	72	135
Paul McKechnie[P], Scotland	72	67	139

Hillside		1 July	
John Singleton[P], England	72	66	138
Christopher Hanson[P], England	69	69	138
Oscar Floren[P], Sweden	67	71	138

Sunningdale New		1 July	
Matthew Southgate, England	70	64	134
Byeong-Hun An, Korea	69	66	135
Chris Rodgers, England	67	72	139

Woburn		1 July	
Paul Dunne*, Rep. of Ireland	67	67	134
Oliver Fisher, England	67	70	137
Rhys Enoch[P], Wales	70	68	138

*Denotes amateur [P]Qualified after play-off

AFRICA

Joberg Open	6-9 February

George Coetzee, South Africa
Justin Walters, South Africa
Jin Jeong, Korea

THE OPEN QUALIFYING SERIES SOUTH AFRICA 2014

Exempt Competitors

Phil Mickelson returns the Claret Jug to Peter Dawson

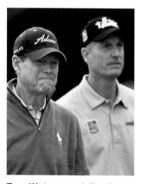

Lee Westwood

Tom Watson and Jim Furyk

Martin Kaymer

Name, Country	Category
Kiradech Aphibarnrat, Thailand	16
Thomas Bjørn, Denmark	5,6
Jonas Blixt, Sweden	5
Grégory Bourdy, France	6
Keegan Bradley, USA	5,11,13,15
Angel Cabrera, Argentina	15
Rafael Cabrera-Bello, Spain	8
Paul Casey, England	6
Roberto Castro, USA	13
Ashley Chesters*, England	25
KJ Choi, Korea	5
Stewart Cink, USA	1,2,3
Darren Clarke, Northern Ireland	1,2,3
Erik Compton, USA	5
Ben Curtis, USA	1
John Daly, USA	1
Jason Day, Australia	5,13,15
Brendon de Jonge, Zimbabwe	13,15
Graham DeLaet, Canada	5,13,15
Luke Donald, England	5,7,13
Jamie Donaldson, Wales	5,6
Victor Dubuisson, France	5,6
Jason Dufner, USA	5,11,13,15
David Duval, USA	1
Ernie Els, South Africa	1,2,3,6,15
Harris English, USA	5
Matt Every, USA	5
Sir Nick Faldo, England	1
Gonzalo Fernández-Castaño, Spain	6
Ross Fisher**, England	5
Tommy Fleetwood, England	6
Rickie Fowler, USA	5
Jim Furyk, USA	5,13
Stephen Gallacher, Scotland	5,6
Sergio Garcia, Spain	5,6,13
Branden Grace, South Africa	6,15
Bill Haas, USA	5,13,15
Chesson Hadley, USA	5
Todd Hamilton, USA	1,2
Padraig Harrington, Republic of Ireland	1,2
David Hearn**, Canada	5
Russell Henley, USA	5
JB Holmes, USA	5
Billy Horschel, USA	13
David Howell, England	6
Mikko Ilonen, Finland	6
Ryo Ishikawa**, Japan	5
Freddie Jacobson, Sweden	5
Thongchai Jaidee, Thailand	6
Miguel Ángel Jiménez, Spain	5,6
Dustin Johnson, USA	5,13
Zach Johnson, USA	4,5,13,15
Matt Jones, Australia	5
Martin Kaymer, Germany	5,6,9,11,12
Hyung-Sung Kim, Korea	20
Chris Kirk, USA	5
Masanori Kobayashi, Japan	19
Brooks Koepka, USA	5

Name, Country	Category
Matt Kuchar, USA	5,12,13,15
Anirban Lahiri, India	5
Pablo Larrazábal, Spain	8
Paul Lawrie, Scotland	1
Marc Leishman, Australia	15
Justin Leonard, USA	1,3
Shane Lowry, Republic of Ireland	8
Joost Luiten, Netherlands	5,6
Sandy Lyle, Scotland	1
Hunter Mahan, USA	4,5,13,15
Matteo Manassero, Italy	6,7
Hideki Matsuyama, Japan	4,5,15,20
Graeme McDowell, Northern Ireland	5,6,9
Rory McIlroy, Northern Ireland	5,7,9,11
Phil Mickelson, USA	1,2,3,4,5,10,13,15
Yusaku Miyazato, Japan	21
Francesco Molinari, Italy	4,5,6
Ryan Moore, USA	5
Kevin Na, USA	14
Bradley Neil*, Scotland	23
Koumei Oda, Japan	21
Thorbjørn Olesen**, Denmark	5
Louis Oosthuizen, South Africa	1,2,3,5,15
Ryan Palmer, USA	5
DA Points, USA	13
Ian Poulter, England	4,5,6
Patrick Reed, USA	5
Justin Rose, England	5,6,9,13
Brett Rumford, Australia	6
Charl Schwartzel, South Africa	5,6,10,13,15
Adam Scott, Australia	4,5,10,13,15,17
John Senden, Australia	5
Webb Simpson, USA	5,9,13,15
Brandt Snedeker, USA	5,13,15
Jordan Spieth, USA	5,13,15
Kevin Stadler, USA	5
Scott Stallings, USA	5
Henrik Stenson, Sweden	4,5,6,13
Richard Sterne, South Africa	6,15
Kevin Streelman, USA	13
Brendon Todd, USA	14
Peter Uihlein, USA	6
Dawie van der Walt, South Africa	18
Jimmy Walker, USA	5
Nick Watney, USA	13
Bubba Watson, USA	5,10
Tom Watson, USA	3
Boo Weekley, USA	13
Lee Westwood, England	4,5,6
Mark Wiebe, USA	22
Bernd Wiesberger, Austria	6
Chris Wood, England	6
Gary Woodland, USA	5,13
Tiger Woods, USA	1,2,3,4,5,12,13,15
YE Yang, Korea	11

*Denotes amateur   **Denotes reserve

Ernie Els and Adam Scott

Bubba Watson

Graeme McDowell and Shane Lowry

Sir Nick Faldo

Key to Exemptions from The Open Qualifying Series

Exemptions for 2014 were granted to the following:

(1) The Open Champions aged 60 or under on 20 July 2014.

(2) The Open Champions for 2004-2013.

(3) The Open Champions finishing in the first 10 and tying for 10th place in The Open Championship 2009-2013.

(4) First 10 and anyone tying for 10th place in the 2013 Open Championship at Muirfield.

(5) The first 50 players on the Official World Golf Ranking for Week 21, 2014, and additional players taken in ranking order from Weeks 26 and 27 as further places become available.

(6) First 30 in the Race to Dubai for 2013.

(7) The BMW PGA Championship winners for 2012-2014.

(8) First 5 European Tour members and any European Tour members tying for 5th place, not otherwise exempt, in the top 20 of the Race to Dubai on completion of the 2014 BMW International Open.

(9) The US Open Champions for 2010-2014.

(10) The Masters Tournament Champions for 2010-2014.

(11) The PGA Champions for 2009-2013.

(12) The PLAYERS Champions for 2012-2014.

(13) The leading 30 qualifiers for the 2013 TOUR CHAMPIONSHIP.

(14) First 5 PGA TOUR members and any PGA TOUR members tying for 5th place, not exempt, in the top 20 of the PGA TOUR FedExCup Points List for 2014 on completion of the 2014 Travelers Championship.

(15) Playing members of the 2013 Presidents Cup Teams.

(16) First and anyone tying for 1st place on the Order of Merit of the Asian Tour for 2013.

(17) First and anyone tying for 1st place on the Order of Merit of the Tour of Australasia for 2013.

(18) First and anyone tying for 1st place on the Order of Merit of the Southern Africa PGA Sunshine Tour for 2013.

(19) The Japan Open Champion for 2013.

(20) First 2 and anyone tying for 2nd place on the Official Money List of the Japan Golf Tour for 2013.

(21) First 2 and anyone tying for 2nd place, not exempt at the conclusion of OQS-Japan Mizuno Open, in a cumulative money list taken from all official 2014 Japan Golf Tour events up to and including the 2014 Japan Tour Championship.

(22) The Senior Open Champion for 2013.

(23) The Amateur Champion for 2014.

(24) The US Amateur Champion for 2013.

(25) The International European Amateur Champion for 2013.

(26) The Mark H McCormack Medal (Men's World Amateur Golf Ranking) winner for 2013.

(23) to (26) were only applicable if the entrant concerned was still an amateur on 17 July 2014.

The Venue

A Course for Courage

By Andy Farrell

"Blown upon by mighty winds; breeder of mighty champions."

Today's elite golfers may only half agree with Bernard Darwin's famous words. After experiencing Hoylake only twice since the course returned to The Open Championship rota after a hiatus of 39 years, there is no doubting the quality of the Champions added to Royal Liverpool's roll of honour.

Tiger Woods in 2006 and Rory McIlroy in 2014 both fit into the category of being one of the finest players of their generation, along with past Champions JH Taylor, Walter Hagen, Bobby Jones and Peter Thomson.

Yet in both these two modern Opens, the wind was not much of a factor, although this year those competitors in the second half of the draw probably had the worst of it, relatively, with the breeze getting up on Thursday afternoon and something more of a wind tickling the links on Friday morning.

Competitors at the Women's British Open in

Heart of The Open: the 18th and tented village.

2012 could legitimately claim to be better qualified about the meteorological perils of the Wirral after the gales and rain storms that swept in from the Irish Sea that year. Whenever the hills of north Wales, so picturesque across the Dee Estuary when the sun shines, disappear, you are in trouble. It even snowed during the 1936 Open — "delightful July weather," wrote Henry Longhurst. In 1956, in the early days of televised golf, Longhurst found himself marooned in the rain up a tower, whose protective tarpaulin had been blown away, and with score sheets that disintegrated on touch. "In the end, we got almost as much sympathy as the players," he wrote.

Though the threat of a thunderstorm hung in the air on Saturday, remarkably still conditions prevailed for much of the 143rd Championship. "It's a great course, a very fair course," McIlroy said of his first Open visit to Hoylake. "We didn't play it in its hardest conditions this week and that's why the scores were quite low." His winning score of 271 was only one adrift of the 18-under-par total posted by Woods eight years earlier.

A far greater contrast lay in the look of the links,

which in the heatwave summer of 2006 had been yellowy-white in appearance. "It's a fantastic test of golf," Woods said after his victory, "and being this firm and fast, it lent itself to amazing creativity." Notably, Woods used his driver only once and manoeuvred his way around the links with a superb display of long- and mid-iron play, even holing a 4-iron second shot at the 14th hole in the second round.

Many months of rain in the build-up to the 2014 Open meant a very different looking links, startlingly green in places, but immaculate nevertheless. With more severe rough, there was a genuine penalty for missing the fairway, while the greens could hardly be called "receptive," even though they were not as bouncy as in 2006.

To witness the 12th Open Championship to be staged here was to be reminded again of Darwin's assertion that, "at Hoylake, the golfing pilgrim is emphatically on classic ground." The club was founded on the site of a racecourse in 1869 and has been at the forefront of the game ever since. Here, both the Amateur Championship and the English Amateur Championship originated, while in 1921 teams made up of amateurs from the USA and Great Britain met in an informal precursor to The Walker Cup. Taylor won his fifth Open title here in 1913 and Thomson his third in a row in 1956. Sandy Herd became the first winner to use a Haskell rubber-core ball, in

Officials checking the third green prior to the start of play.

The par-3 13th hole with the Dee Estuary and the Welsh hills behind.

1902, while Arnaud Massy became the first and only Frenchman to win The Open, in 1907, and Fred Daly the first of four Irishmen, in 1947.

Uniquely, two members of Royal Liverpool are among the three amateurs to have won The Open, and the third, Jones, won his third title at Hoylake in his Grand Slam year of 1930. Harold Hilton won his second Open when Hoylake staged its first in 1897. Hilton was a flamboyant character who regularly swung himself almost off his feet, and his cap off his head, and had many interests within the game. He was the founding editor of *Golf Monthly*, whose present editor is also a member of Royal Liverpool but who was firmly in a watching brief for this Open.

John Ball was the son of one of the founding members of the club — the manager of the Royal Hotel, which served as the original clubhouse — and went on to win The Open in 1890 as well as the Amateur Championship eight times. In contrast to Hilton, he was a reserved man who combined power and grace into a meticulously precise game. After one victory, he nonchalantly revealed the key to his success: "I was hitting my drives the right height for the day," he said.

On a remarkable occasion in 1907, after the St Andrews Day Medal

> ## It's a
> # Fact
>
> The lowest score in an Open at Royal Liverpool is higher than for any other course currently used for the Championship. The Open record of 63 has been scored at Turnberry, Muirfield, St Andrews, Royal Birkdale and Royal St George's, while 64s have been scored at Royal Troon, Carnoustie and Royal Lytham & St Annes. The best score of 65 scored at Hoylake was recorded by Tiger Woods, Ernie Els, Chris DiMarco and Sergio Garcia in 2006 and matched by Dustin Johnson, Chris Wood, Shane Lowry, Marc Leishman and Jim Furyk in 2014.

Sunrise over Hoylake: the majestic clubhouse of Royal Liverpool Golf Club.

had been cancelled due to fog, Ball went out to play anyway. He had accepted a bet that he could not better a score of 90, play within two-and-a-quarter hours, and use only one ball. Not only did he not lose his ball, which was black for good measure, he beat the time limit and scored an 81. The following week, when the competition was re-scheduled in more playable conditions, Ball was among those who shared the title on a score of 82.

Peter Ryde, Darwin's successor as golf correspondent of *The Times,* wrote that it was inherent in the nature of the links that "Opens at Royal Liverpool are won by courage more than brilliance."

Of course, it helps to have both, but often there is adversity to be overcome before claiming the Claret Jug. Hagen had to pull himself together after going to the turn in 41 strokes in the final round before winning in 1924, while six years later Jones had a 7 at the par 5 in the far corner of Hoylake, then the eighth hole, after taking five to get down from just short of the green. "It was the most inexcusable hole I have ever played," he said. "An old man with a croquet mallet could have got down in two. I will play that hole over a thousand times in my dreams." A lesser man might have lost his head; Jones rallied to claim the second leg of

his "Impregnable Quadrilateral."

No one showed more courage, or brilliance, than Roberto de Vicenzo in winning The Open, after a host of near-misses, at the age of 44 in 1967. He did so while holding off the challenge of Jack Nicklaus and with a famous shot at what was then the 16th hole, the par 5 around the edge of the members' practice ground, or the "Field" as it was known. His drive finished five yards short of the shallow bank bordering the out-of-bounds. From there his second shot needed to be played with a spoon over the corner of the Field that juts into the fairway. With Nicklaus claiming a birdie just ahead of the Argentinian, a matching 4 was required.

"A mistake at that point could cost Vicenzo what, at his age, had to be a last chance of achieving his greatest ambition," wrote Pat Ward-Thomas in *Not Only Golf.*

"I doubt that any such frightening thoughts plagued his mind. He struck the shot as promptly and decisively as he always did; he was never a fidget. The ball thundered away over the Field and not for an instant was it going to finish anywhere but in the heart of the green. The rest was academic."

Ward-Thomas added: "Vicenzo, the look of an emperor about him, strode into the amphitheatre by the last green towards a reception the like of which I had never heard before. Its sustained warmth and affection were tribute to a fine human being as well as to a great golfer and a victory nobly won."

At the same hole on Saturday of the 2014 Championship, McIlroy produced a modern equivalent when his towering 5-iron set up his second eagle in three holes. As in 2006, the course numbering was changed from the members' regular layout so that it ended on this renowned par 5 and started at the old 17th, where a new green, 40 yards in length, angles away from the fairway.

This makes for a stern start to the round, with the traditional opener, which doglegs around the other side of the Field in front of the clubhouse, now used as the third. At least that prevents a player repeating the fate of Harry Vardon in hitting his first two shots of the 1902 Open out of bounds. Amazingly, the six-time winner still led after the first round.

It also makes for a dramatic finale to the course, with two par 5s in the last three holes and the space for a modern amphitheatre to be built around the 'new' 18th, with a spectacular wraparound horseshoe grandstand producing a wonderful atmosphere at the final green.

As McIlroy, who had displayed both brilliance and courage in fending off his last-day pursuers, marched triumphantly into the arena to a rapturous ovation at the end of a memorable week, it was hard to disagree with another of Darwin's claims that, "there is always a rich reward at Hoylake for the man who can play his approaches really straight and with a firm, sure touch."

 What I really like about Royal Liverpool is that well-struck shots are rewarded and poorly struck shots are penalised. And that's not always the case in links golf.

—Phil Mickelson

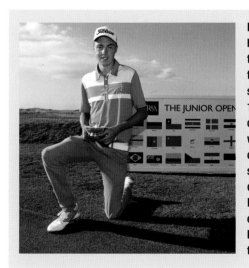

Ireland's Kevin Leblanc became the first winner of the week when he claimed the Junior Open Championship at West Lancashire. The 15-year-old from The Island club, near Dublin, closed with a 74 to finish on a five-over-par total of 221 and one stroke ahead of Teodoro Soldati, of Italy, and Belgium's Diane Baillieux. The biennial event will next take place at Kilmarnock Barassie during the week of the 2016 Open.

A NEW WAY OF VIEWING THE OPEN

By Peter Dixon

The first thing you notice if you sit in a stand at The Open Championship with a tablet 'streaming' information from around the course is that you have suddenly attracted a raft of new friends. You have key information at your fingertips and are required, in the nicest possible sense, to share some of it.

Sitting overlooking the first tee at Royal Liverpool on the opening day of the 143rd Open Championship was to experience the oldest and most coveted of all the Majors from a new and different perspective.

For the first time, The R&A encouraged tablets and smartphones to be used at the Championship. And, if personal experience is anything to go by, the move proved to be an overwhelming success. At £1.5 million to install, the Wi-Fi network that covered the whole of Hoylake did not come cheap, but it allowed The Open experience for spectators to be moved onto another level entirely.

"We did debate this at great length, as you could imagine," said Peter Dawson, Chief Executive of The R&A, who was acutely aware of potential problems, but trusting of fans not to disturb the players in front of them. Headphones, earphones and the 'mute' key were the order of the day.

"The great thing about coming to The Open Championship now is that you can watch these wonderful players live in front of you and get the atmosphere of what's going on elsewhere on the course," Dawson added. "The drawback of watching live golf is that you can't see what's going on elsewhere." No longer.

With an all-singing, all-dancing Open App available to download free of charge, it was possible to keep abreast of all that unfolded on Hoylake's wonderful links. The breadth and variety of what was on offer, from virtually any point on the course, was simply tremendous. What, one wonders, would Willie Park Sr, winner of the first Open in 1860, have made of it all? The mind boggles.

After fielding the almost inevitable question — "How's Tiger doing?" (Answer: "He's played better.") — it was time to put the

system fully to the test. Moving to the stand behind the 16th green gave a perfect illustration of how best to use the technology. With earphones in, you could observe players putting-out in front of you (Paul Casey is one that springs to mind), while at the same time watching on live TV those teeing-off behind (that man Tiger, for instance). And if you wanted to hear, say, Peter Alliss' take on the way play was progressing, it was there at the touch of a screen.

The options were many and varied. You could read up on individual players, follow them as they manoeuvred around the course, and get instant feedback on their rounds. How, for instance, was Matteo Manassero's splendid first round of 67 made up? Answer: seven birdies, two in the first three holes, two bogeys and nine pars.

Checking on Manassero was one way of filling the gap between Rory McIlroy's approach shot at the 16th on the first day and the eventual Champion's exquisite bunker shot from the side of the green. A little while later and you could watch McIlroy's birdie at that hole on the highlights package that was continually being updated or, for that matter, Manassero's post-round interview.

It was impossible to say which of the features was most impressive. Nothing, it seemed, had been left to chance. You could read the timeline on the right side of the screen, made up of bite-size chunks of information and key-moment video clips, or read the tweets that were coming in from around the course and beyond. Or you could switch to @TheOpenLive, The Open's very own TV channel for all that was going on behind-the-scenes, turn to BBC Radio 5 Live for their on-course commentaries, or listen to The Open's own radio station.

It would be easy to sit in one spot and not move. However, the absolute charm of The Open is in walking the course and soaking up the atmosphere. In this instance, you could go to the far end of Hoylake, sit around the back of the 10th green, and miss nothing.

The author sharing information with his new-found friends.

It did not end there, however. For the first time, electronic leaderboards were used on each of the first 17 holes. Tradition dictated that the iconic yellow scoreboards remained in place on both sides of the grandstands surrounding the 18th green, but the information being given to those walking the course, or sitting behind the other greens, was a huge improvement on what had gone before.

As each group approached a green, the individual scorecards were displayed, along with detailed information on each of the players and how they were actually playing (fairways hit, greens in regulation, number of putts, and so on). You could see where a player stood in relation to the field, follow the action from elsewhere on the course, and even watch highlights on the screen.

"The way that people now embrace this technology is something that golf also has to embrace. And that's exactly what we're doing. I think the spectators are going to feel a great benefit this year," Dawson had said on the eve of the event. How right he was.

First Round
17 July 2014

All Eyes on Rory

By Andy Farrell

McIlroy takes the lead on 66 by one from Manassero in ideal conditions on the opening day at Hoylake.

As he walked to the first tee on a calm, warm opening morning, the question was, exactly which Rory McIlroy would be turning up for the 2014 Open Championship? Focused prodigy or unpredictable genius? Or, to put it another way, would he be more Tiger Woods or Phil Mickelson?

McIlroy has said himself that he struggles to be as intense at every tournament as Woods was in his prime, not least in the way the 14-times Major Champion plotted his way around Hoylake to win the 2006 Open. There are times when the Northern Irishman does not know what is going to happen from one day to the next. Mickelson can be just as erratic. Even in winning The Open at his 20th attempt, in 2013, there were many ups and downs at Muirfield until Lefty's brilliant late charge of

Rory McIlroy tees-off at the par-3 ninth.

four birdies in the last six holes.

About the only consistent feature of McIlroy's 2014 season had been his inconsistency. Just the week before arriving at Hoylake, he had opened with a 64 in the Scottish Open at Royal Aberdeen only to score a 78 the next day. At Jack Nicklaus' Memorial Tournament he had done something similar, which had the Golden Bear berating the curly-haired one like an exasperated, yet kindly, uncle with the words: "How the hell can you shoot 63 and then 78?"

Such extremes of scoring hint at a game with which neither Nicklaus nor Woods are familiar, and yet McIlroy can also produce moments of greatness that mark him out as a worthy successor to that pair as the dominant player in the game. The 2011 US Open at Congressional, when McIlroy won wire-to-wire, and the 2012 US PGA Championship at Kiawah Island were two such occasions, while his victory in the BMW PGA Championship, from seven strokes back, at Wentworth in May, was an important boost to confidence and morale.

As always at the start of an Open, conjecture was high on how a number of players would perform:

❶

A gorgeous morning for golf as David Howell teed-off at the first hole to get the 2014 Open under way.

Ivor Robson, Open starter for a 40th year, with Peter Dawson.

Mickelson in defence of his title; Woods in his first Major of the year following back surgery; Martin Kaymer after winning the US Open at Pinehurst in McIlroy fashion, by eight strokes and from wire-to-wire; Justin Rose after winning his last two tournaments, including the Scottish Open the previous Sunday; Adam Scott, the world number one after near-misses in The Open in the previous two years; Sergio Garcia on the return to the scene of one of his near-brushes with the Claret Jug.

But from the moment McIlroy striped a 2-iron down the first fairway, all eyes were on the 25-year-old Ulsterman. His approach shots at the first three holes were no more than five feet away, and though he missed birdie chances at the first and the third, he could not miss at the second hole.

McIlroy had 191 yards for his second shot and hit one of his majestic, towering 6-iron shots that finished four inches from the hole. Now this was not the bone-hard, baked out links of 2006, or of Muirfield in 2013, but even a little more rain the previous day had not left the very green greens anything like soft, and the ability to land such high shots so delicately is a special skill indeed. "It was a really nice shot," McIlroy reflected. "That's the advantage of having a high ball-flight on a links when there's no wind, you're able to bring it down like that and stop it close to the pin."

He added: "We had perfect scoring conditions out there this morning, there wasn't much wind early on. I hit some really good shots on the first few holes

Where's Woods? Tiger makes his way through the crowd on the way to a 69.

First Round Leaders

HOLE	1	2	3	4	5	6	7	8	9	10	11	12	13	14	15	16	17	18	TOTAL
PAR	4	4	4	4	5	3	4	4	3	5	4	4	3	4	3	5	4	5	
Rory McIlroy	4	(3)	4	4	(4)	(2)	4	4	3	(4)	4	(3)	3	4	3	(4)	4	5	66
Matteo Manassero	(3)	4	(3)	4	5	3	4	[4]	(4)	(3)	[5]	3	4	(2)	(4)	4	(4)	(4)	67
Brooks Koepka	(3)	**6**	4	(3)	(4)	(2)	4	4	3	5	4	4	(2)	[5]	3	(4)	4	(4)	68
Edoardo Molinari	(3)	(3)	4	4	5	3	4	4	3	(4)	4	[5]	3	4	3	(4)	4	(4)	68
Francesco Molinari	[5]	4	4	4	(4)	3	4	4	(2)	5	(3)	4	3	[5]	3	(4)	4	**(3)**	68
Jim Furyk	4	4	4	4	(4)	(2)	[5]	4	(2)	(4)	4	4	3	4	(2)	5	4	5	68
Sergio Garcia	(3)	4	(3)	4	(4)	3	4	4	3	[6]	(3)	4	(2)	4	3	5	4	5	68
Adam Scott	4	4	4	(3)	**(3)**	4	4	4	(2)	5	4	[5]	(2)	4	(2)	5	4	5	68
Shane Lowry	[5]	(3)	4	4	5	3	[5]	4	3	(4)	(3)	(3)	3	(3)	3	5	4	(4)	68

Spectators in the tented village were also able to watch the action on the third fairway.

and that gave me the confidence that I could go from there."

Driving is the other strong part of McIlroy's game, and the first time he took out the big stick he smacked it 350 yards down the par-5 fifth, leaving him miles ahead of his playing partners, Hideki Matsuyama and Jordan Spieth. A birdie-4 ensued, and he was confident enough to use the driver again at the seventh, for a safe par at what proved the most difficult hole of the week, and the 11th, where his 373-yarder left him just 20 yards short of the green, though he took three to get down.

The birdies were coming, at the short sixth, from 18 feet, at the long 10th, where he chipped his third shot to within two feet of the hole, and at the 12th, from 15 feet, where he took the lead at five under par. Matteo Manassero birdied the last for a 67, but then McIlroy got up and down from a bunker at the 16th to get to six under. He was also in a greenside bunker at the last, but had to settle for a two-putt par and a round of 66. He had not dropped a shot, something only Ryan Moore and Thomas Bjørn, with a pair of 70s, also achieved.

McIlroy led on the first day of The Open in 2010 at St Andrews, when he opened with a 63. "It is a similar golf course in that you need to take advantage of the par 5s," he said. "The game plan is actually quite similar — stay out of the bunkers. The 63 at St Andrews was a better round of golf, but this was solid. I birdied three of the four par 5s and took my pars on the tougher holes.

"There are quite a few holes on the back nine that are right-to-left doglegs, which suits my natural shot shape. And I don't feel like you're too restricted in your approach shots. The greens are quite generous, quite flat, and you can be quite aggressive with your second shots. Obviously, I like to play the game that way."

At 25, he was the senior citizen of his grouping. The 22-year-old Matsuyama, who had recently won the Memorial Tournament for his first win in America, scored a 69, and Spieth, already a PGA Tour winner at the age of 20, a 71. McIlroy agreed he would be playing a lot of golf with the pair over the next decade or so, but added: "I'm sort of getting past that 'young guy' stage, I think."

Japan's Koumei Oda scored a 69 as did compatriots…

…Yoshinobu Tsukada…

…and Hideki Matsuyama.

The trio from Japan had plenty of support.

Few could disagree. Three days later, no one did.

Manassero, at 21 still a young gentleman of Verona, had not made the cut at The Open since his debut as the Amateur Champion in 2009 at Turnberry. After hitting into a bunker from the first tee, he splashed out and then holed a 9-iron from 160 yards for a birdie-3. It was a nice start that would lead to a trio of Italians on the leaderboard, with the Molinari brothers, Edoardo and Francesco, both scoring 68s. It was Edoardo's first Open appearance for three years, during which time he had undergone separate operations on his left wrist and then, just when he had got back to playing full-time, his left thumb.

It was, in the words of David Howell, a "gorgeous morning" for golf. He should know, having hit the first tee shot at 6.25am. He set his alarm for 4.15 and woke up naturally at 4.11. "I thought, 'Shall I go for four more minutes?' No. I got up," he said. "Being The Open Championship, as soon as you wake up you remember what you're doing and the adrenaline kicks in." Howell returned a 72, while there was a 69 for one of his playing partners, the

Matteo Manassero

The Italians
"It's good for the kids watching at home"

Italy hasn't had much to cheer in The Open Championship aside from Costantino Rocca's play-off loss to John Daly in 1995 at St Andrews. Matteo Manassero and the Molinari brothers, Edoardo and Francesco, tried to make up for that in the opening round of the 143rd edition of golf's oldest Major.

Manassero arrived at Hoylake fresh from a fourth-place finish in the Scottish Open at Royal Aberdeen. Needless to say, he was sufficiently ready for the challenges of links golf.

"It was the best preparation I could have had," Manassero said. "We had strong wind, little wind, calm wind the last day. We had different directions of wind and the course was firm. It was real 'linksy,' so I just put myself in a very links frame of mind."

The 21-year-old Italian got into the mix with a five-under-par 67 to take the early lead before Rory McIlroy eclipsed him with his own 66. Manassero took advantage of calm conditions. He made seven birdies and dropped just two shots, at the ninth and 12th holes. He did most of his damage on the back nine, with five birdies, including all three par 5s.

"This golf course exposes itself on the par 5s," said Manassero, winner of the 2009 Amateur Championship. "Every par 5 was reachable today. It's a big bonus if you can birdie a lot of them, because they're not such tough holes."

Edoardo Molinari

The Molinari boys helped the Italian cause with matching four-under-par 68s. Elder brother Edoardo made five birdies and dropped just one shot, a bogey at the par-4 12th hole. It was just the score he was looking for after watching weather forecasts. "With the weather coming in for the next few days, it was very important to shoot a good number today," Edoardo said. "You can play a little bit more defensively, if you need, in the next few days."

Francesco began his round poorly and ended it spectacularly. He bogeyed the first, then found birdies at the fifth, ninth and 11th holes, before dropping a shot at the 14th. He more than made up for that slip with a birdie at the 16th and an eagle at the 18th. Two 3-woods and an 18-foot putt took care of the finishing hole.

"It's a golf course that I think won't play as easy as it did today," Francesco said. "On a day like today you just want to make some birdies and you want to be as close to the top as possible."

Italian golf suffered a bit of a lull after Rocca. In Manassero and the Molinaris they have three bona fide challengers for the Claret Jug in the coming years. "We are three talented guys that work hard, so we're bound to get the results," Francesco said. "It's good to see three Italians up there. I'm sure it's going to be good for the kids watching us at home."

Francesco Molinari

—**Alistair Tait**

Sergio Garcia drives at the par-5 16th hole with Luke Donald and Rickie Fowler looking on.

equally likeable Robert Karlsson.

Karlsson was the European number one in 2008, but only two years ago had to withdraw on the eve of The Open at Royal Lytham & St Annes because he feared he could not take the club away at address. The demons have faded over time and form has slowly returned, but sometimes it is the little things in life that matter. Nothing buoyed the Swede more on this particular morning than to rise after his 4am alarm to find his wife Ebba already cooking breakfast.

Garcia is something of a new man since his last visit to Hoylake, which did not end well. Playing in the final pairing with Woods in 2006, both his choice of outfit — canary yellow from head to toe — and his play could have been vastly improved. His own memories of that week instead linger on the 9-iron second shot he holed at the second hole in the third round.

American Brooks Koepka hits his second shot at the fifth.

At the first hole this time he had a 9-iron in his hands again, and this time his shot hit the flagstick and finished two feet away. "I always remember my hole-out, so it was a funny moment with the same club," said the Spaniard. He birdied the first, the third and the fifth, chipped in at the 11th, after dropping a shot at the previous hole, and birdied the short 13th from 18 feet. A 68 put him alongside the Molinaris, American Brooks Koepka, in his second Open, and Jim Furyk, in his 19th, from among the early starters.

Garcia was in a friendly grouping with Luke Donald, who was not at his best in a 73, and Rickie Fowler, who lay just behind the Spaniard on 69. "It was fun to be able to feed off each other," said the young American. Garcia was revelling in the atmosphere, too. "You always come with a different frame of mind at this Championship," he said. "I love it so much and I enjoy the people out here. It's almost like a Ryder Cup when people start shouting, 'Come on, lads!' It's good to hear."

Shane Lowry, on his way to a 68, drives at the 17th hole late in the day.

Billy Horschel just misses a putt at 18.

Woods was another of the morning starters and he joined the group on 69, but only after a shaky start. He bogeyed the first hole of the Championship in 2006, but bogeys at the first two holes this time was hardly in the script. Then again, who knew what the script was? The 38-year-old had hardly played since undergoing back surgery in March and he was forced to miss the Masters and the US Open before going on to miss the cut in his only tournament prior to arriving in Britain.

A good putt for par at the fourth seemed to settle him down, and the putter swung into action as of old when he birdied five holes out of six on the back nine. "It felt good to be back out there competing," Woods said. "It wasn't exactly the greatest of starts, but then I turned it around." At least he finished with all his clubs intact. On the 17th, playing partner Henrik Stenson, who scored a 72, put his gap wedge over his thigh and snapped it in two before calmly handing the remains to his caddie, Gareth Lord, who accepted the offering as if it were a routine matter.

Mickelson got too close to the tented village when his second shot at the 18th ran out of bounds. A bogey at the last meant a 74,

Round of the Day: **Rory McIlroy – 66**

Noteworthy

- **Hole 2**: 2-iron, 6-iron, one putt from four inches
- **Hole 5**: Driver, 9-iron, two putts from 30 feet
- **Hole 6**: 6-iron, one putt from 18 feet
- **Hole 10**: 3-wood, 5-iron left of green, chip to two feet, one putt
- **Hole 12**: 3-wood, 8-iron, one putt from 15 feet
- **Hole 16**: Driver, 6-iron, bunker shot to three feet, one putt

McIlroy makes his sixth birdie of the day from a bunker at the 16th.

"McIlroy either set himself up for a good run at the Claret Jug or another dose of Friday failures. In what already has been an unusual year for golf, no trend is more mysterious than Boy Wonder going from awesome to awful overnight."

—**Doug Ferguson,** *Associated Press*

"Woods looked close to unstoppable by the end as he proved that his stated expectation to hold the Claret Jug for a fourth time on Sunday was no mere fancy."

—**Oliver Brown,** *The Daily Telegraph*

"The question of what McIlroy does on a Thursday night has been raised. The answer — a kickabout in the garden with a couple of friends and dinner with his parents."

—**Neil Squires,** *Daily Express*

"The cavalry is tucked in behind. Prominent among them is the world number one Adam Scott. For all the Australian claimed a Major Championship in the form of last year's Masters, his career will never be complete without atonement for an Open collapse in 2012."

—**Ewan Murray,** *The Guardian*

"Stay indoors, Britain," warned the Met Office. Not a chance. Tiger's putter was firing up its own heatwave on the greens."

—**Paul Mahoney,** *The Independent*

Amateur Ashley Chesters was the leading Englishman on 70.

Sir Nick Faldo hits his tee shot at the fifth hole.

not quite how he hoped to go about retaining the Claret Jug. Characteristically optimistic afterwards, he said: "Certainly the score sucks, but my game is as good as it has been in a long time."

It was a trying day for a vaunted trio in the afternoon wave. Alongside Mickelson, Bubba Watson, who won his second Masters title in April, found too many bunkers during a 76, while Ernie Els, who won his second Open title two years earlier at Lytham, opened with a 79. The South African had a distressing start when he pulled his opening tee shot into the crowd and a spectator was hit on the chin.

"It wasn't nice, there was blood everywhere," Els said. "Hurting the guy the way I did, I felt pretty bad. I was quite rattled." The 60-year-old spectator required stitches for the cut but was otherwise none the worse. Watson and Mickelson noticed Els was out of sorts, and he missed a drag-back tap-in on the first green on the way to a triple-bogey. At seven over after seven holes, his Championship was over before it had got going.

With the breeze getting up in the afternoon, scoring was higher for the second half of the draw, with only three of the 18 sub-70 rounds coming later in

> **I tried to tell Ernie that I do that all the time [hitting a spectator] but it didn't help.**
> —Phil Mickelson

First Round Scores	
Players Under Par	48
Players At Par	17
Players Over Par	91

Rickie Fowler was three behind McIlroy after a 69.

Phil Mickelson begins his title defence at the first tee.

"Matteo Manassero was right up there; so too were the flying Molinari brothers. This was the biggest Italian move since Pavarotti made an assault on the all-you-can-eat buffet. Ahead of them, though, a Northern Irishman was enjoying La Dolce Vita."

—Nick Rodger, *The Herald*

"On the other end of the scale, where the tragic storylines dwell, Royal Liverpool exacted its pound of flesh."

—Peter Richmond, *USA Today*

"Many warned him to delay his return to action, but the idea that Woods would voluntarily relinquish the opportunity to play in The Open Championship was fanciful. If Woods feels he has a sniff, he will give it a go."

—Matthew Syed, *The Times*

"Hoylake was braced for the return of the King but Phil Mickelson's first round as defending Champion was hardly a glorious celebration — in fact at times it was hard not to feel a little sorry for him."

—Chris Cutmore, *Daily Mail*

"Tiger Woods' pursuit of Jack Nicklaus' all-time record of 18 Majors started out as a childhood ambition and evolved into a genuine pursuit. But, in more recent years, it has run into a dead end. He is locked on a number and can't move on."

—Philip Reid, *The Irish Times*

Justin Rose chips at the 16th green and has to settle for a par.

the day. Kaymer, who had a wonderful May and June, winning The Players Championship as well as the US Open, struggled to a 73, while Jason Day appeared to hurt his wrist playing from the rough, having only just recovered from a thumb injury.

Rose came in with a 72, which meant that the leading Englishman was Ashley Chesters, the 2013 European Amateur Champion. The 24-year-old from Shrewsbury posted a 70 in the morning, but the one advantage Rose had in teeing-off in the afternoon was time to be reunited with his driver. Upon arriving at the course in the morning, Rose found another driver, of the same model but different specifications, in his bag. It was one of two that should have gone to a friend of his caddie, Mark Fulcher. Instead, his own driver had ended up in Bedford, 190 miles away, and had to be driven back to

Adam Scott tees-off at the 14th hole, set in the sand dunes by the Dee Estuary.

the course. It arrived with Rose on the third hole, which was okay because he had not been planning on using it until the seventh. "You have to see the funny side," he admitted.

Rose was playing with Scott, who produced the day's best front nine, a 31 that included birdies at the fourth and the ninth and an eagle at the fifth. Strangely, both the day's best nines were produced in the afternoon, with Shane Lowry coming home in 32 as he and Scott joined the group on 68.

Having set out knowing the target McIlroy had posted, Scott said: "It was important to keep pace with Rory. He has the potential to really put his foot down. We've seen him win Majors by eight, and there is nothing stopping him from shooting a low round again tomorrow."

Nothing except McIlroy himself. Just the second question in his press conference concerned his second-round struggles — or "Freaky Friday" as some were calling it — which started when he almost missed the cut at the Masters and continued with bad starts to his second rounds at Quail Hollow and Sawgrass. Only three times in 13 events in 2014 had he scored lower than in the first round, while there was no forgetting the 80 that followed his opening 63 at St Andrews in 2010.

"Maybe I'm just going out with higher expectations on a Friday after shooting a low round," he said. "I've just got to try and put those expectations aside and take it one hole at a time."

Easier said than done.

Low Scores	
Low First Nine	
Adam Scott	31
Low Second Nine	
Shane Lowry	32
Low Round	
Rory McIlroy	66

It's a Fact

Before 2014, 11 players that led outright after the first round went on to win The Open; 13 more who shared the first-round lead also won. Rory McIlroy would go on to become the seventh Champion to lead outright after every round, following Ted Ray, 1912; Bobby Jones, 1927; Gene Sarazen, 1932; Henry Cotton, 1934; Tom Weiskopf, 1973, and Tiger Woods, 2005.

1

McIlroy plays his bunker shot at the 18th green.

Round One Hole Summary

HOLE	PAR	YARDS	EAGLES	BIRDIES	PARS	BOGEYS	D.BOGEYS	OTHER	RANK	AVERAGE
1	4	458	0	16	89	46	4	1	5	4.263
2	4	454	0	7	97	45	7	0	3	4.333
3	4	426	0	22	108	24	2	0	12	4.038
4	4	372	0	27	113	15	1	0	14	3.936
5	5	528	4	66	65	15	5	1	17	4.705
6	3	201	0	15	113	25	3	0	8	3.103
7	4	480	0	5	94	43	13	1	1	4.429
8	4	431	0	19	111	22	4	0	10	4.071
9	3	197	0	22	114	19	1	0	13	2.994
OUT	**35**	**3,547**	**4**	**199**	**904**	**254**	**40**	**3**		**35.872**
10	5	532	3	70	74	6	3	0	18	4.590
11	4	391	0	25	100	28	2	1	11	4.064
12	4	447	0	15	89	44	6	2	4	4.308
13	3	194	0	21	103	31	1	0	9	3.077
14	4	454	0	9	95	42	7	3	2	4.359
15	3	161	0	17	101	33	5	0	7	3.167
16	5	577	1	49	89	15	2	0	16	4.795
17	4	458	1	10	106	34	3	2	6	4.218
18	5	551	5	46	79	16	6	4	15	4.897
IN	**37**	**3,765**	**10**	**262**	**836**	**249**	**35**	**12**		**37.474**
TOTAL	**72**	**7,312**	**14**	**461**	**1,740**	**503**	**75**	**15**		**73.346**

FROM FACTORY FLOOR TO OPEN DREAM

By Lewine Mair

Thursday was the best day of John Singleton's life and he would say precisely the same of Friday. "I shot six over and it felt like six under," commented the 30-year-old local factory worker after his opening 78. "I've played in The Open and that's something I will always be able to say."

Singleton was no Maurice Flitcroft, the crane driver notorious for trying to gatecrash The Open in the 1970s. Where Flitcroft's background was of hitting shots on a beach while walking his dog, Singleton was a good enough golfer to have won a scholarship to a junior college in the United States and to have tried his hand on sundry US mini-tours. Alas, his progress was interrupted by a series of knee problems and, when the money ran out, he was forced to return home to Wallasey and find himself a job.

He felt he had been lucky to get his post at Advanced Electrical Varnishes in Birkenhead. Among his duties, he drives a fork-lift truck

and makes batches of thick resin for waterproofing. And in between times, as his colleagues would mischievously report, he is wont to pick out a club from an old golf bag and have a knock-about with a ball made from squashed cling film.

Singleton had been at the company for over a year when this second chance at golf came along. The Open was to be played just up the road at Hoylake and his fiancée, Lucy Johnson, encouraged him to give it a try. After he scraped through Regional Qualifying at Mere, he moved on to Final Qualifying at Hillside. Once again, it was tight. After a closing 66 in regulation play, he was one of three survivors from a four-way play-off. His dream of playing in The Open was now a reality.

The top players have their teams around them — coaches, managers, trainers — and Singleton had his. Only, in his case, the team included 30 workmates and a managing director, Jonathan Kemp, who not only gave everyone the day off so they could watch him play, but paid for their tickets as well.

Kemp had a beer with Singleton on the eve of the Championship and told him: "I don't think I've ever wanted someone not to come

back to work on a Monday, but in your case I would be happy." It was a reference to how, if things went well, Singleton might be able to resume his golf career.

Singleton had a practice round with Justin Rose during which the 2013 US Open Champion advised: "Focus, forget the crowd, and take everything slower."

The advice was not easy to follow when, at 10.32 on Thursday morning, he was standing on the first tee for real. Friends, new-found fans, workmates and fellow members of Eastham Lodge Golf Club were there, too. As it turned out, some were not quite as well prepared as he was. At one point, they called for Singleton to throw them his tube of sunscreen lotion. He obliged, although not without issuing a cheerful reminder that he was playing in The Open. Meanwhile, you could see that Peter Uihlein and Marc Warren, his playing partners, were as happy for Singleton as he was for himself.

When Singleton followed a bogey at the ninth with a birdie at the 10th, he was well placed on level par. Thereafter, though, he dropped six shots to finish on six over. People questioned if nerves had played a part. They had — and Singleton suspected it had been inevitable. "This is The Open and it's at home," he said. "It's the biggest tournament in the world. Of course I was going to be nervous; I was close to tears."

As much as anything, he had set out to make the most of the experience: "I'm still one of the select few who get to play, so I tried to enjoy every moment." And what made that easier was the contribution of the supporting cast: "Every shot I hit, every step I took, someone was shouting nice things."

After signing his card, Singleton did as many interviews as the first-round leader, while his fiancée waited patiently outside. At more than eight months' pregnant, she must have been worrying lest the baby put in an appearance before he did.

A second round of 70 was not quite enough to make the cut — he finished two strokes off the cut line, on four over par — but his closing four holes were something to celebrate: birdie, birdie, par, birdie. First, he drained a long putt at the short 15th. Next, there was a thriller of a 16th, played via a spectator pathway, where a fan shook him warmly by the hand before advising, "Just concentrate on the shot, John." He did just that, chipping to six feet and sinking the putt for birdie. After a par at the 17th, he bisected the 18th fairway before threading his second shot through the guardian bunkers. He missed the putt for eagle, but tapped in for his 4.

The crowd around the green gave him a grand reception and that was when the floodgates opened for Singleton. "They're good memories," he said.

Good memories for everyone who was at The Open of 2014.

Second Round
18 July 2014

No More 'Freaky Fridays'

By Andy Farrell

A second 66 in a row gives McIlroy a four-stroke lead over Johnson despite the American's course record.

There was a Saturday feeling about Friday's play in the 2014 Open Championship. With the scoreboard changing little in the morning and the leaders playing late into the evening, it was as if we had gone straight to the third round. Perhaps this was why Rory McIlroy failed to succumb to his recent second-round woes and instead continued his march towards the Claret Jug in commanding fashion.

The only thing freakish about this Friday was how the wind died down late in the afternoon while the Northern Irishman was still on the course. How well he took advantage, continuing his expectation-free progression from the previous day and yet knowing precisely how he was standing in relation to the field.

On the 18th green, where a large gallery remained

This Friday Rory McIlroy kept heading in the right direction.

as the evening cooled after a day of intense summer heat, McIlroy holed a putt from just over five feet for a birdie. It was an emphatic end to a round that began less certainly but left him at 12 under par, the target he had set himself during the back nine. He still could not quite better his score of the day before, but a second successive 66 had propelled McIlroy to a four-stroke lead over Dustin Johnson.

His halfway total of 132 was the same as that posted by Tiger Woods on the way to victory in 2006. Woods was 14 strokes adrift this time and only just made the cut on the two-over-par qualifying mark. Though he also made a birdie on the last hole, to make it to the weekend after a triple-bogey at the 17th had put his continuation in the Championship in peril, it was a clearing-the-stage moment. Others were demanding the attention. In the following group, Charl Schwartzel finished with three birdies in a row for a 67 that put him in joint third place, at six under, alongside Francesco Molinari, Ryan Moore, Rickie Fowler, Sergio Garcia and Louis Oosthuizen.

Then came McIlroy, an imperial air about him already after conquering his Friday phobia, and

Rickie Fowler kept up his pursuit of McIlroy with a second successive 69.

Low Scores

Low First Nine

Dustin Johnson	32
Thorbjørn Olesen	32

Low Second Nine

Rory McIlroy	33
Dustin Johnson	33
Ryan Moore	33
Marc Warren	33
Jimmy Walker	33
Victor Dubuisson	33
Paul Dunne*	33
David Howell	33
Graeme McDowell	33
John Daly	33
Patrick Reed	33

Low Round

Dustin Johnson	65

Johnson, who set the best score of the week, a 65 that equalled the lowest round in an Open at Hoylake. The American had seven birdies and was the only player in the field not to have a bogey during the round. Still to come was Victor Dubuisson, the Frenchman eventually matching McIlroy's 66.

Scotland's Marc Warren returned a 68 to lie at five under par and second in the home challenge behind McIlroy, an achievement put straight into perspective by the death the same evening of Bob Torrance, coach of his son Sam, Warren and many others from the top to the bottom of the game. The mournful news contrasted with the joyous scenes back at the 18th as John Singleton, a local factory worker, signed off with a 70 to the cheers of friends and colleagues. And not to forget another moment of history for Tom Watson as the 64-year-old former Champion broke his own Open record as the oldest known player to make the cut. It seemed as if all the day's crucial action had been compressed into the last few hours.

McIlroy's round did not get under way until 2.27pm, by which time, after a morning of 20mph winds, no one had dislodged him from the top of the leaderboard. A bogey at the first hole might have

Second Round Leaders

HOLE	1	2	3	4	5	6	7	8	9	10	11	12	13	14	15	16	17	18	TOTAL
PAR	4	4	4	4	5	3	4	4	3	5	4	4	3	4	3	5	4	5	TOTAL
Rory McIlroy	5	4	4	4	4	2	4	3	3	4	4	4	3	4	2	5	3	4	66-132
Dustin Johnson	3	4	3	4	4	3	4	4	3	4	3	4	3	4	3	5	3	4	65-136
Francesco Molinari	5	3	3	4	4	3	4	6	4	4	4	4	2	3	3	5	4	5	70-138
Ryan Moore	4	5	4	4	5	3	5	3	2	4	4	4	2	4	3	5	3	4	68-138
Rickie Fowler	4	5	4	3	4	3	4	4	3	4	4	5	3	4	3	4	3	5	69-138
Sergio Garcia	5	2	5	4	4	3	4	4	3	4	4	4	3	5	3	5	4	4	70-138
Charl Schwartzel	3	4	4	4	4	3	4	5	2	4	3	4	3	6	3	4	3	4	67-138
Louis Oosthuizen	3	4	4	4	4	3	4	4	3	4	4	3	4	3	3	5	5	4	68-138

Dustin Johnson matched the low Open round at Hoylake with a 65.

"McIlroy brilliantly dismissed all that guff about a Friday Hoodoo with a majestic second successive round of 66 at Hoylake."

—Karl MacGinty, *Irish Independent*

"Woods' second-round 77 at Royal Liverpool was a reminder that this is a 38-year-old man coming off back surgery and not the 24-year-old who in 2000 won the US Open by 15 strokes and the 'British' Open by eight to complete the career Grand Slam."

—Ron Sirak, *Golf Digest*

"There was a 10-shot improvement in his score, which on first glance appears very impressive. The only thing is, Bryden Macpherson shot a second-round 80, which sort of tells you how bad Thursday was."

—Jim McCabe, *Golfweek*

"Never mind Freaky Friday, this was phenomenal Friday for Rory McIlroy. The Northern Irishman has laid the demons to rest and his rivals know exactly how they feel."

—James Corrigan, *The Daily Telegraph*

"In all, 13 Englishmen fell and six survived, led by Justin Rose and, more surprisingly, David Howell. With both men at two under after shooting rounds of 70, it would be deeply ambitious to predict a quick end to the 22-year wait for an English winner."

—Riath Al-Samarrai, *Daily Mail*

Phil Mickelson recovers from the rough at the fifth to claim an eagle.

hinted that he had spent the morning brooding over his inability to back up a low score, but today was different. "Even though I started a little shaky with that bogey, I was still confident that I had some chances coming up," he said.

Another big drive at the fifth set up a birdie-4 and then he hit an 8-iron to seven feet at the short sixth. Panic over, all things — driver, irons, putter — were working as they should. Even a pheasant wandering across the eighth green could not distract him from holing another seven-footer, and a 4 at the 10th gave him a fourth birdie in six holes.

Rolling in the putt at the sixth, getting under par for the day, and improving on his overnight six-under-par score had been, he said, the crucial moment. "Once I got to seven, I felt, 'Okay, this time I feel good. I can get to eight. I can get to eight, nine, 10, 11, 12.'"

And so he did, with a late burst of three birdies in the last four holes, kick-started by an 8-iron to under three feet at the short 15th. At the 17th he changed tack from the day before and belted his driver 390-odd yards to within chipping range of the green. He made

Francesco Molinari and Ryan Moore shake hands after both finish at six under par in a share of third place.

light of it, saying Johnson, in the group behind, had put it 10 yards nearer the green, but it was another telling blow. It told of the high quality of his execution, but also what he would describe as an "inner peace."

"I am very comfortable in what I am doing right now," he explained. "It is hard to describe and I wish I could get into it more often. It all comes down to if you are confident with your game and you are in control of your ball, it makes things a lot easier."

He added: "I've always said, whenever you play this well, you always wonder how you've played so badly before. And whenever you've played so badly, you always wonder how you play so well. Golf is a very fickle game."

As for 'Freaky Friday,' McIlroy said: "My second rounds this year have been terrible and there isn't

Jimmy Walker missed his putt at 15 and finished at four under.

Sergio Garcia holes his 6-iron shot at the second hole for an eagle-2 before celebrating with Luke Donald.

really an explanation. But hopefully I put it to bed today."

A McIlroy runaway was the last thing the morning starters wanted given they had the worst of the conditions on each of the first two days. George Coetzee was the only player from this half of the draw to feature in the top 18 after two rounds. A 69, his first sub-70 round in The Open since his debut at Sandwich in 2011, left him at five under, alongside Warren and Jim Furyk. When the South African finished his round, he was tied for second with Matteo Manassero, whose second round was yet to begin.

Coetzee briefly shared the top spot on the leaderboard by getting to six under with a wonderful run of three birdies in a row. He holed from 40 feet for a 2 at the 13th, made a 12-footer for a 3 at the 14th, and hit a 6-iron shot to two feet at the 15th. Did he see his name on the scoreboards? "I think it's obvious I looked as soon as I was at the top," he said, "because I made two bogeys right after that." But there was a closing birdie with which to celebrate his 28th birthday. "To have my birthday coincide with my favourite Major is nice," said the South African.

Justin Rose tangled with the rough on the fourth hole.

Jim Furyk swayed his way to five under par.

Zimbabwean Brendon de Jonge, 34 this day, was experiencing the treat for the first time, although his maiden Open ended in missing the cut despite a 70, while Sir Nick Faldo's 57th birthday also included a missed cut in what was his 36th Open appearance.

Justin Rose and Adam Scott were among those hoping to make a morning charge before their efforts stalled in the wind. Scott bogeyed the second and third holes on the way to a 73, while Rose posted a 70 to move to two under. There was the sense of a round that had got away from the 2013 US Open Champion. He chipped in twice from 60 feet at successive holes, the ninth for birdie and the 10th for eagle, but dropped a stroke at the 14th after taking a penalty drop from a bush. "That little stretch around the turn, and I also made a nice putt on eight for par, would be a turning point if I go on to win. But all it's done right now is give me an opportunity to go into the weekend," Rose said. "It

Charl Schwartzel salutes the gallery during his 67.

2

Round of the Day: **Dustin Johnson – 65**

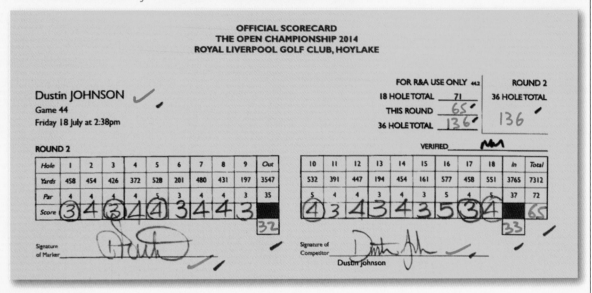

OFFICIAL SCORECARD
THE OPEN CHAMPIONSHIP 2014
ROYAL LIVERPOOL GOLF CLUB, HOYLAKE

Dustin JOHNSON ✓
Game 44
Friday 18 July at 2:38pm

	FOR R&A USE ONLY 442	ROUND 2
18 HOLE TOTAL	71	36 HOLE TOTAL
THIS ROUND	65	
36 HOLE TOTAL	136	136

VERIFIED ___ ΛΛ

ROUND 2

Hole	1	2	3	4	5	6	7	8	9	Out
Yards	458	454	426	372	528	201	480	431	197	3547
Par	4	4	4	4	5	3	4	4	3	35
Score	③	4	③	4	④	3	4	4	3	32

Hole	10	11	12	13	14	15	16	17	18	In	Total
Yards	532	391	447	194	454	161	577	458	551	3765	7312
Par	5	4	4	3	4	3	5	4	5	37	72
Score	④	3	④	3	4	3	5	③	4	33	65

Signature of Marker _____

Signature of Competitor _____
Dustin Johnson

Noteworthy

- **Hole 1**: Driver, 5-iron, one putt from 10 feet
- **Hole 3**: 4-iron, pitching wedge, one putt from five feet
- **Hole 5**: Driver, sand wedge into right bunker, up and down
- **Hole 10**: Driver, 6-iron, two putts from 20 feet
- **Hole 11**: 3-iron, lob wedge, one putt from 12 feet
- **Hole 17**: Driver, lob wedge, one putt from four feet
- **Hole 18**: Driver, 4-iron over green, putt on, one putt from eight feet

It's a **Fact**

Sandy Lyle made his 39th appearance in The Open in 2014, putting him seven behind Gary Player, 46, but one ahead of Sandy Herd and Jack Nicklaus on 38. Tom Watson made his 37th appearance and, at the age of 64, extended his own record as the oldest known player to make the cut. The five-time Champion has now played all four rounds 26 times.

Johnson was in fine driving form.

Not distracted by a pheasant playing through, McIlroy still birdied the eighth.

feels right now we are on the wrong side of the draw." A television nearby showed the flag at the second hole completely limp. "I don't like to see the flag doing that," Rose said. "When I was playing the second, it was howling. Whenever you come off the golf course, it feels calmer than when you had to play. We'll see."

At two under par, Rose was still only four behind at the time but ended the day 10 shots adrift. He and David Howell were now leading the English challenge, while 24-year-old amateur Ashley Chesters missed the cut after a 77. With Ireland's Paul Dunne and Cheng-tsung Pan, of Taiwan, having finished on four over par, and Scotland's Bradley Neil out of the running, Chesters needed three birdies in the last four holes to make the cut and win the Silver Medal as the leading amateur. He managed two, at the 15th and 17th, but could only par the two closing par 5s.

Phil Mickelson had his usual eventful round, but a 70 left the defending Champion only at level par. He bogeyed the third, almost holed his approach on the fourth after hitting into the crowd with his tee shot, eagled the fifth, missed a chance on seven, bogeyed the eighth, lost a ball at the 10th but saved par after hitting a 2-iron to six feet, hooked a 5-iron against the wind to four feet at the 17th but whiffed the putt, and birdied the last via the left grandstand. "It's really close to being good," he said.

Birthday boy George Coetzee on the 18th, where he made his sixth birdie of the day.

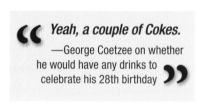

Yeah, a couple of Cokes.
—George Coetzee on whether he would have any drinks to celebrate his 28th birthday

Second Round Scores	
Players Under Par	38
Players At Par	14
Players Over Par	103

Instead it was Johnson who made the biggest charge of the day. Starting out at one under par, he birdied the first from 10 feet, the third from five feet, and got up and down from a greenside bunker for a 4 at the fifth. His outward half of 32 was matched only by Thorbjørn Olesen, of Denmark. Then he came home in four-under 33, which was matched by McIlroy and a host of others. He birdied the 10th and the 11th, then the 17th, where his huge drive left only a short pitch to four feet, and the last.

Impossible as it was to keep pace with McIlroy, the American still found himself two ahead of everyone else. "I couldn't be happier with the position I'm in," he said. "I thought it was really tough out there today, so to shoot seven under was a very good score around here."

Woods, Ernie Els, Chris DiMarco and Garcia were the players to score a 65 during the 2006 Open at Hoylake. Garcia's effort came in the third round, when he holed his second shot at the second with a 9-iron.

Remarkably, at the second hole on Friday he holed his approach shot again. This time it was with a 6-iron though from slightly closer to the hole. "In 2006 the hole was playing downwind," he explained. "Today it was 162 yards straight into a hard wind, but it's another great memory to have on that hole."

Garcia celebrated by throwing his arms wide open and slapping

The Old Man of the Links

How long will Tom Watson carry on playing such good golf at such a high level and how many more records can he break while doing so? After nearly winning the 2009 Open at the age of 59 years and 10 months, we hailed his performance at Turnberry with laudatory adjectives such as "ageless," "evergreen," "stunning," "remarkable," and "astonishing."

Three years later, at Royal Lytham & St Annes, he broke the record Bob Charles had set at the same club in 1996 by becoming the oldest man to beat the halfway cut at The Open. Watson was then two months short of his 63rd birthday. In 2014, two months short of his 65th birthday, he extended his own record by reaching the last two rounds of The Open for the 26th time.

How does he keep on doing it? In part it is down to his determination. On Friday he had a bad run from the seventh, when he dropped three strokes in four holes. "I hit some lousy shots in mid-round and when I was three over I told myself I had better play some good golf. And I did," he said. A second 73 put him on 146, the same mark coincidentally as Stewart Cink, among others, who had beaten him in a play-off at Turnberry five years earlier.

To those who watched him, Watson had given a master class in the art of playing links golf. "Links golf is all about distance control," Watson said. "Can you get the right distance? Can you play the chess game? Move your ball to this position to get to that position? It's not how far you drive the ball, it's how straight you hit the ball."

The way he plotted his passage up the 18th hole was a perfect demonstration of this approach. He knew he was close to the cut line, so he didn't do anything fancy. A safe drive to the right of the fairway was followed by a 4-iron over the practice ground that left him a pitch to the green. "This was old man's golf," Watson said. "I hit it to the right, I hit it to the left, and I hit it onto the green. There's no age when I'm out there. I'm doing the same thing as I did when I was 22, although I can't hit the ball very hard any more."

It doesn't seem to matter. Watson won Opens when he could hit the ball a long way and he plays well in them when he can't hit the ball so far. He is a wonder.

And thanks to The R&A extending the five-time Champion's exemption by a year, he will have a chance to break his own record again at St Andrews next year. One last hurrah on the Swilcan Bridge is no more than the old man of the links deserves.

—John Hopkins

---

hands with playing partners Fowler and Luke Donald. His was one of three eagle-2s on the day. Wales' Rhys Enoch drove the green at the 11th hole, which was playing at 389 yards for the day, and had only a tap-in of two feet for his 2, although a triple-bogey at the next undid his chances of making the cut. And Japan's Masanori Kobayashi holed his second shot at the 14th, just as Woods had done in the second round in 2006.

It was at the 14th that Garcia got hot and prickly. His eagle was sandwiched between bogeys at the first and third holes, but he birdied three of the par 5s and dropped his only other shot at the tricky par 4 near the estuary. He drove into a bush and donned waterproofs as protection to play his recovery. "It was quite warm and I still got stung on the leg, so hopefully I've learnt my lesson. I won't hit it there again," he said.

Garcia and his family had spent Thursday evening watching the *Seve* movie, which may or may not have helped the Spaniard to keep fighting himself out of trouble in his second-round 70 in true Ballesteros

 I don't know where I'm going to be when I'm 64. If I was playing the quality of golf that Tom Watson is playing, then I'd be very, very pleased.

—Darren Clarke

Neither leaderboard nor scorecard made good reading for Miguel Ángel Jiménez, who missed the cut.

> ❝ I prefer it when it's very difficult. And that is what The Open is about. It's about grinding it out and being happy when you make a par. ❞
>
> —Martin Kaymer

> ❝ I'll be dead honest with you, 25 of these a year would probably drive me out of the game. But I like coming over two or three weeks a year and playing links golf. ❞
>
> —Jim Furyk

Francesco Molinari plays a bunker shot at the 18th green as he posted a 70.

style. "I don't know if it inspired me to play today the way I did," Garcia reflected, "but obviously it is very inspiring to watch. My father knew him when he was quite young, so it was nice to watch it on film. I recommend everybody to watch it."

Fowler kept pace with his playing partner thanks to birdies at the 16th and 17th holes getting him to six under par. The 25-year-old posted a second successive 69 despite feeling that his putting was sub-standard because "my eyes were a bit off." He meant that he found it hard to get the line of the putts. "You're so focused on trying to start it on line, you forget about the pace you are trying to hit it," he said.

Moore, his compatriot, made six birdies in his last 11 holes in his 68 and felt, with his low ball flight, that he was beginning to figure out links golf. Francesco Molinari took over as the leading Italian after a 70, while his brother slipped back with a 73, as did Manassero with a 75.

But all the discussion was still about McIlroy.

Victor Dubuisson improved by eight shots with a 66 on Friday.

Louis Oosthuizen returned a 68 to be six under par.

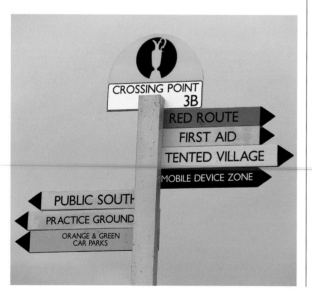

Yusaku Miyazato's first Open only stretched to two days.

"When his driver is on, he's almost unstoppable," said Fowler. "I don't think he has a whole lot of weaknesses. I know he has had a couple of Fridays where he's struggled, but it is easy for the momentum to go the other way if he gets just a little off with his driver and misses a few putts.

"But he is not scared to keep going the way he is. He's definitely going to be tough to catch. I know the weather forecast could throw something into the mix tomorrow. We'll see what happens. But it's fun to go out and battle against him."

If Friday had felt like a Saturday, Saturday was going to be like no day before at The Open Championship. With a severe storm system approaching, which had the potential for lightning strikes for much of the day, The R&A took the unprecedented decision to schedule the third round in threeballs with a two-tee start.

Perhaps only Mother Nature could stop McIlroy now?

Round Two Hole Summary

HOLE	PAR	YARDS	EAGLES	BIRDIES	PARS	BOGEYS	D.BOGEYS	OTHER	RANK	AVERAGE
1	4	458	0	21	96	32	7	0	8	4.160
2	4	454	1	9	84	58	4	0	2	4.353
3	4	426	0	9	117	29	1	0	10	4.141
4	4	372	0	16	105	32	3	0	10	4.141
5	5	528	4	75	56	19	2	0	18	4.615
6	3	201	0	4	105	44	3	0	4	3.295
7	4	480	0	8	89	49	9	1	1	4.404
8	4	431	0	13	91	41	6	4	3	4.335
9	3	197	0	9	103	39	4	0	5	3.245
OUT	**35**	**3,547**	**5**	**164**	**846**	**343**	**39**	**5**		**36.677**
10	5	532	7	62	69	16	1	0	17	4.626
11	4	391	1	31	99	23	1	0	15	3.948
12	4	447	0	17	105	31	1	1	12	4.123
13	3	194	0	16	102	36	1	0	9	3.142
14	4	454	1	17	89	41	6	1	6	4.239
15	3	161	0	16	104	31	2	2	7	3.161
16	5	577	1	33	96	21	4	0	14	4.961
17	4	458	0	28	100	22	2	3	13	4.052
18	5	551	1	62	63	20	9	0	16	4.832
IN	**37**	**3,765**	**11**	**282**	**827**	**241**	**27**	**7**		**37.084**
TOTAL	**72**	**7,312**	**16**	**446**	**1,673**	**584**	**66**	**12**		**73.761**

THE GREAT UNKNOWN... TIGER RETURNS

By Art Spander

What is golf other than possibilities and memories? The game lingers. The years gather. We think of then and try to equate it to now, attempting to stop time, more difficult than stopping a 3-wood shot on a small, hard green.

You can't go home again. It was the title of a Thomas Wolfe novel, but little known is that Wolfe asked permission to use the line after he heard it in conversation with the writer Ella Winter. Too often we misunderstand the thought. We literally may return home, but we can't return to what we were, what we knew.

What we knew at Royal Liverpool when The Open Championship returned there in 2006 after a gap of 39 years was a course scorched by the sun and, by the end of the Championship, also by Tiger Woods. Hoylake, Royal Liverpool, and Woods were forever linked — in record books and, maybe more, in the mind's eye.

There was so much about Tiger as the 2014 Open began, first that he actually was competing, because at the end of March he underwent lumbar microdiscectomy surgery on a pinched nerve and a question mark hung over his summer schedule; second, having entered only one prior event, the Quicken Loans National at Congres-sional, at the end of June, not even he knew the state of his game.

Even healthy, or as healthy as limited news from the Woods camp indicated, Tiger had struggled in Major Championships in recent years, including the 2013 Open at Muirfield where, beginning the last round only two shots off the lead, he came home with a 74 that left him five back of Champion Phil Mickelson. Tiger's last win in a Major was the 2008 US Open.

The Great Unknown found some form, or so we — and Woods — believed when he shot a three-under-par 69 in the first round at Hoylake. Stunning, in a way. Also misleading. Friday brought Woods, and those waiting for that 15th Major, back to earth. All too quickly. The first round, he began bogey, bogey, and then looked and performed decently. But an afternoon start on day two was of no advantage.

Using a driver — remember, in 2006 he utilised the club only once in four rounds — Woods hooked into the deep stuff left of the first fairway. He grabbed two clubs from his caddie Joe LaCava and then chopped away with one of them. His fourth swing got him to the green, and a nifty two-putt produced a double-bogey-6.

"I didn't hit the driver very good today," he would say candidly, because he certainly did not. Then why the driver and not a 3-wood? "I couldn't carry the bunkers," said Woods, who in 2006 didn't try or need to carry the bunkers.

After a bogey at the second, Woods had 14 straight pars. Not what is required to win, but at least consistent. And guaranteed to make the cut. Then an improbable reversion.

A ball out of bounds at 17, a triple-bogey, and now he was above the cut line. But there was a little of the old Tiger in the new Tiger. Forced to make a seven-footer for his only birdie of the day to get to play in the third round, Woods did exactly that. After his second-worst score in a Major as a professional — he had that 81 in the wind and rain at Muirfield in 2002 — Woods was both disappointed and cheered.

"It gives me a chance," he said. "Hopefully I can do something like Paul did in '99." That's when Paul Lawrie came from 10 strokes off the third-round lead to tie after Jean Van de Velde hit into a burn and took a triple-bogey on the 72nd hole. Lawrie beat Van de Velde and Justin Leonard in a play-off.

When play was switched to a two-tee start on Saturday, Woods had the same 11.01am time as leader Rory McIlroy — off last, like the old days. But McIlroy was starting at one, Tiger at 10.

"Made a lot of mistakes," was the Woods mantra after day two, emphasising the obvious. Before the bitter end, Tiger would have a total of two triple-bogeys and three doubles.

Perhaps Tiger was surprised. Perhaps not. Three former Major Champions, Curtis Strange, Andy North and Paul Azinger, commenting for ESPN, the American sports network, were not at all surprised.

"I hope he makes the cut," Strange, a back-to-back US Open winner, said of Woods before play began. "I hope he hits solid shots, I hope he progresses. But I don't think you could ever expect him to be on the first page of the leaderboard come the weekend. And that's just from common sense.

"That's talking about the great Tiger Woods. If it was Paul [Azinger], Andy [North] or me — normal people — I'm not even sure we would go over there."

Tiger came. He and we learned past was not necessarily prologue.

Third Round
19 July 2014

Where Eagles Dare for Rory

By Andy Farrell

Patience rewarded as McIlroy bursts into a six-shot lead after being caught by Fowler.

Not even Mother Nature could beat Rory McIlroy at the 2014 Open Championship. McIlroy may not have been in control of the weather but he appeared to be in control of everything else, and that included taking advantage of the benign conditions on the third day at Hoylake.

It was a historic day for The Open Championship with a two-tee start in operation for the first time in its 143rd staging. There was heavy rain for those teeing-off at 9am — Keegan Bradley, Jason Dufner and Phil Mickelson at the first and, unprecedentedly, Grégory Bourdy, Chris Rodgers and Ben Martin at the 10th — but it soon abated and a warm, still, oppressive day ensued. The links was there for the taking, but there was always the sense of waiting for the storm to hit.

It duly did, about the time in mid-afternoon when the halfway leaders would normally have been teeing-off for their third rounds. It was the way that McIlroy finished that provided the day's drama. Two eagles over the last three holes, the only 3s at either 16 or 18 all day, extended his overnight lead of four strokes to a 54-hole advantage of six.

By the time the torrential rain returned, the Northern Irishman had escaped to the interview tent to do battle with the noise of the downpour on the canvas roof. The only thing more thunderous all day — given that the threat of lightning thankfully never materialised — was the ovation afforded McIlroy at the 18th green. "I got goosebumps from how loud it was," he said. "The support from the crowds this week has been absolutely fantastic. I said I wanted to give them something to cheer for."

He had done just that with his play on the 551-yard finishing hole. When in full flow McIlroy plays with an abandon usually only found in the Ryder Cup fourballs, except he does it without the safety net of a partner already in good shape. A perfect drive left him 237 yards from the flag, and another superbly hit 5-iron, soaring high over the corner of the out-of-bounds and safely out of reach of the greenside

Rory McIlroy stayed No. 1 thanks to his eagle at the 18th.

Third Round Leaders

HOLE	1	2	3	4	5	6	7	8	9	10	11	12	13	14	15	16	17	18	TOTAL
PAR	4	4	4	4	5	3	4	4	3	5	4	4	3	4	3	5	4	5	TOTAL
Rory McIlroy	5	4	4	4	4	3	4	4	3	5	3	5	3	3	3	3	5	3	68-200
Rickie Fowler	3	3	4	4	4	2	5	4	3	4	3	3	3	5	3	6	5	4	68-206
Sergio Garcia	5	3	4	4	4	3	4	3	2	5	4	4	3	4	3	4	5	5	69-207
Dustin Johnson	3	4	4	5	5	3	5	5	4	5	4	4	2	4	2	5	4	4	71-207
Victor Dubuisson	4	5	3	4	4	2	3	4	3	5	4	3	4	4	3	5	4	4	68-208
Edoardo Molinari	3	3	4	4	5	3	5	4	3	4	4	3	4	4	2	5	4	4	68-209

History at the 10th tee

"On the tee, Grégory Bourdy." The words were the same as ever, the voice and the location were different. For the first time in the history of The Open there was a two-tee start in operation for Saturday's third round. And because Ivor Robson, The Open starter for the last 40 years, could not be in two places at once, Rules Official Mike Stewart did the honours at the 10th tee.

Stewart, a senior tournament director for the European Tour, was having dinner in Harrogate with his in-laws on Friday evening when David Rickman, The R&A's Chief Referee, phoned to explain his change in role for the following morning.

The last time Stewart acted as an official starter was at the Wang Four Stars tournament at Moor Park in the 1980s, although a few years ago he filled in for the first group of the morning at the South African Open at Pearl Valley when the official starter, one I. Robson, was prevented from arriving on time by a transportation issue. "I had to remind Ivor this was not the first time I had stepped in for him," Stewart joked.

As well as announcing the players, the starting duties include helping to make sure players exchange scorecards, have no more than 14 clubs in their bag, and tee-off on time. With half the 36-hole qualifiers having to be transported out to the 10th to start their rounds, the logistics might have proved tricky, but in the event the latest a player arrived was eight minutes prior to their tee-time.

"It was a pleasure to do and an experience I'll never forget," Stewart said. "A bit surreal, but I was happy to help out. I had no idea about the significance until people kept telling me I'd made history."

A forecast that included the threat of thunderstorms for much of Saturday was the reason for the revised schedule. "All the professional advice we are receiving tells us that significant disruption is highly likely," Rickman said on Friday night.

Although lightning did not delay play during the third round, the players were supportive of the decision. "When someone told me last night we were going to have a two-tee start, I used some naughty language and called them a liar, but they were correct," said 2011 Champion Darren Clarke. "It was slightly different because we've never done it at The Open, but they had to do it today and they made the perfect call."

As torrential rain hammered down on the interview tent, almost drowning out his post-round press conference, Rory McIlroy also approved of the decision. "It's the second best decision The R&A has made this year," said the Northern Irishman. "The first being bringing The Open back to Portrush."

—Andy Farrell

bunkers, pulled up just 11 feet short of the hole. There are putts that simply demand to be holed, and McIlroy could sense that this was just such an occasion. "I felt like those two shots into 18 deserved an eagle," he explained. "I wanted to finish it off the right way."

Five shots ahead or six, what did it matter? Actually, quite a lot. Never had a player lost The Open when six or more strokes ahead with a round to play — Tiger Woods in 2000 at St Andrews was the last to be as many as six ahead after 54 holes. But twice players with a five-stroke lead had lost — Macdonald Smith, at Prestwick in 1925, and Jean Van de Velde, at Carnoustie in 1999.

Rickie Fowler made a birdie from the sand at the 18th for a 68.

Low Scores	
Low First Nine	
Shane Lowry	31
Low Second Nine	
Graeme McDowell	32
Low Round	
Darren Clarke	67
Jordan Spieth	67

Dustin Johnson birdies the 15th hole during his 71.

Not that McIlroy knew his history out in the cauldron of Hoylake's 18th green. He was just working on instinct. "The way I look at it, six shots is better than five," he said. "I just wanted to try and be as many ahead as I possibly could. That's why I was grinding over that putt at the last."

It was a remarkable turnaround since he had walked off the 12th green after a bogey only tied for the lead with Rickie Fowler. Seven birdies in 12 holes from the American had turned what many feared would be a runaway victory for the two-time Major Champion into a duel of the 25-year-olds. But three late bogeys from Fowler, combined with the turbo-charged finish from McIlroy, appeared decisive. "I was conscious of Rickie getting a little closer, so it was nice to be able to come up with the goods when I needed them over the last few holes and restore that lead," McIlroy said.

It had looked unlikely for much of the day but both finished it with scores of 68, leaving McIlroy at 16 under par — his 54-hole total of

Jim Furyk, who finished at six under par, chipping at the seventh.

"McIlroy is 18 holes away from becoming the third-youngest player in history to win the first three legs of the career Grand Slam. A couple of guys named Nicklaus and Woods are the only ones to have done it quicker."

—Ron Green Jr, *Global Golf Post*

"His reaction to being caught was almost explosive. As Fowler drew level, McIlroy sprinted."

—Stephen Jones, *The Sunday Times*

"Fowler finally is equipped to counterpunch consistently. Before this year, he was more hat than cattle, as they say in Texas."

—Jeff Rude, *Golfweek*

"Garcia admitted afterwards that playing McIlroy in this kind of form is as daunting as waging war against Woods in his prime; an almost futile exercise however well those in the chasing pack might be playing."

—Matt Lawton, *Mail on Sunday*

"The official whose job it is to engrave the winner's name on the Claret Jug could be forgiven for getting started."

—Paul Forsyth, *Scotland on Sunday*

"McIlroy is trying not to get ahead of himself, even though many have all but handed him the Claret Jug."

—Helen Ross, PGATour.com

Sweden's Robert Karlsson posted a 70 to be six under.

Graeme McDowell came home in a best-of-the-day 32.

200 setting a record for Opens at Hoylake, three strokes better than Woods in 2006. Fowler finished at 10 under par, one ahead of Sergio Garcia, who had a 69, and Dustin Johnson, who scored 71.

Fowler's resurgence since missing the cut in the 2013 Open was striking. It was at the weekend at Muirfield that he got talking to Butch Harmon, coach of that year's Champion Golfer, Mickelson. Fowler had been thinking of employing Harmon as his swing man and it seemed as good a time as any. A high finish at the Masters this year was followed by an even better performance in the US Open at Pinehurst. As at Hoylake, he had got himself into the final pairing on the final day, and though his pursuit of Martin Kaymer was a forlorn one, sharing second place behind the German was his best result in a Major.

Now Fowler was trying to prevent a second successive wire-to-wire Major winner being crowned. But McIlroy at Hoylake was proving every bit as dominant as Kaymer in the Sandhills of North Carolina. This was the fourth time he had led after three rounds of a Major. The first time did not end well as he let a four-stroke advantage fritter away on the back nine at Augusta during the 2011 Masters. At the US Open a couple of months later, however, he led by eight with a round to play and won by eight. At the 2012 US PGA Championship at Kiawah Island, he was three in front after 54 holes and won by eight again. A quick learner.

"I feel very comfortable in this position," McIlroy confirmed. "This is the third night in a row that I'll sleep on the lead. It helps that I've been in this position before and I've been able to convert, to get the job done. I'm really comfortable with my golf game, comfortable with the way I'm hitting it, really comfortable on the greens. I just need to play one more solid round."

Who else would be chasing him? Behind Garcia and Johnson was Victor Dubuisson, on eight under par. The Frenchman had four birdies in five

Rickie Fowler
Ready to be a Major contender

Rickie Fowler's talent and determination have been apparent since, aged 21, he was a captain's pick for the United States side in the 2010 Ryder Cup at Celtic Manor. Four down after 12 holes to Edoardo Molinari in the singles, Fowler birdied his last four holes to secure a half point for his team.

A Californian who once rode dirt bikes, Fowler attended Oklahoma State University and, at most tournaments on the PGA Tour, plays Sunday rounds attired in shirt, trousers and flat-brim hat of bright orange, the university's colours. But he's more than the clothes he wears, particularly now he is under the guidance of coach Butch Harmon.

"The main goal going into the year was to be ready for the Majors and go contend in the Majors," Fowler said in early summer. "I really wouldn't care less what happened in the other tournaments because my main goals were to be ready for the Majors."

He was certainly ready, although preparation did not equate with ultimate success in the first three Majors of 2014. Two shots off the lead going into the final round of the Masters, Fowler closed with a 73 and finished in a share of fifth. At Pinehurst, he made it into the final Sunday pairing of the US Open, but was so far back of Martin Kaymer after 54 holes that his two-over-par 72 was good only for a tie for second with Erik Compton.

In The Open, Fowler had a 68 in the third round on Saturday to force his way into the final pairing for a second successive Major, this time, of course, with Rory McIlroy. The Fowler-McIlroy relationship began when they were opponents at the 2007 Walker Cup at Royal County Down. "We're good buddies," Fowler said. "At the same time we want to beat each other as bad as possible. It was just a matter of time before the two of us found a way to sneak into the final group together."

McIlroy duly snuck off with a well-deserved victory, but a fourth sub-70 score (he had rounds of 69, 69, 68 and 67) gave Fowler his second straight runner-up finish in the Majors, this time alongside Sergio Garcia.

Fowler is also friends and a practice round partner of 2013 Open winner Phil Mickelson, who is a generation older. "I've learned a lot from Phil," Fowler said. "I kind of hate to say this, but he has been like a dad for me. Seeing how he operates, on and off the course, how he treats his fans, he's very well respected. It's a great way to warm up for events and to try to impress him — because Phil is not easily impressed."

Fowler said after the third round that he gave himself room for improvement every day. "Bad swings happen," he confirmed, "but I'm satisfied with where I'm at. All in all, I was swinging great." Indeed he was.

—**Art Spander**

Louis Oosthuzien and Charl Schwartzel help point the way for George Coetzee's tee shot at the 12th.

Marc Warren strikes his second to the third hole.

Edoardo Molinari plays from the rough at the fifth.

holes on the front nine in a 68. Edoardo Molinari also had a 68 and was at seven under, the third different leader in the Italian sub-Championship after his brother Francesco fell back with a 75. Their compatriot Matteo Manassero bounced back from a poor second round with a 68 to lie on six under, alongside Adam Scott, Robert Karlsson, Jim Furyk and Charl Schwartzel. It was not a great day for the South African trio playing together, with Schwartzel's 72 the best of the lot as former Champion Louis Oosthuizen and George Coetzee had a 76 and a 74 respectively.

The best scores of the day were the 67s of Darren Clarke and Jordan Spieth. Having only just made

Matteo Manassero rallied with a 68 after slipping to a 75 on Friday.

the cut, Spieth was out last off the 10th tee with Woods — the same time the leaders were going off the first — and the 20-year-old out-scored the three-time former Champion by six strokes. Clarke also teed-off at the 10th, but by the end of the day he was up to a share of 12th place on five under.

After seven pars in a row, the 2011 Champion birdied the 17th and 18th holes, then the first and the second to make it four in a row. After what he called a "silly three-putt" at the third, he holed a monster putt at the fourth and got a 4 at the par-5 fifth before end-ing the day with four pars. "I played nicely," Clarke said. "The rain was pretty heavy at the start, but we got a break with the weather. It wasn't supposed to be as good as it has turned out to be. There are opportunities out there, but they've hidden a lot of flags away behind bunkers. You can make mistakes very easily if you are not careful."

Almost unanimously, the players respected the precaution of implementing the two-tee start, something that is routine in similar circumstances week-to-week on tour. Everyone got to play in similar conditions, rather than the weather favouring some and not others over a longer day, but the essential challenge of seaside links golf remained — to assess whether birdie, par or bogey might be accept-

"If the meaning of 'bottle' is delivering at the point of greatest demand, then doff your cap to this fellow [McIlroy]. Two eagles over the closing three holes. Come on."

—Kevin Garside,
The Independent on Sunday

"Sergio Garcia would not have been human had he not seen Rory McIlroy disappearing into the distance and thought: 'That could have been me.'"

—Dave Kidd, *Sunday Mirror*

"Dubuisson is an introvert by nature, preferring to escape the glare of the media and happily ignore the lure of fame."

—James Riach, *The Observer*

"Keegan Bradley has fascinated the galleries over the past three days for the way he doesn't so much size up a shot as stalks it — crouching, retreating, and advancing on his ball with the mannerisms of a lion eyeing up a grazing wildebeest."

—Martin Johnson, *The Sunday Times*

"A sharp tap in the privates with a 9-iron could scarcely have brought more tears to the eyes of Fowler as he headed for the 18th tee. Over the previous 40 minutes, he had gone from sharing the lead with McIlroy to trailing the Northern Irishman by five shots."

—Alasdair Reid,
The Sunday Telegraph

Adam Scott was five under for the last eight holes.

able on any hole in any given conditions and get on with it.

A bogey at the first hole for the second day running was not acceptable for McIlroy, given that a poor approach found a bunker on the wrong side to save par. Johnson made a birdie and suddenly the lead was down to two strokes. Though McIlroy would birdie the fifth, Johnson would fail to match him, and bogeys at the seventh, eighth and ninth holes halted the American's challenge there and then.

Instead it was Fowler who made a charge. He hit a wedge shot to four feet at the first and then holed from 30 feet for a second birdie at the next. A birdie-4 at the fifth and a 2 at the par-3 sixth got him to 10 under par, only for a poor drive to cost him a shot at the seventh. He was out in 32, as was Garcia, his playing partner for the third day running. The Spaniard dropped a shot at the first but birdied his favourite hole, the second, and also

Jordan Spieth matched the best score of the day with a 67.

Round of the Day: **Darren Clarke – 67**

Darren CLARKE
Game 14
Saturday 19 July at 9:11am

FOR R&A USE ONLY (R)

36 HOLE TOTAL __144__   ROUND 3 54 HOLE TOTAL
THIS ROUND __67__
54 HOLE TOTAL __211__   __211__

ROUND 3

VERIFIED

Hole	1	2	3	4	5	6	7	8	9	Out
Yards	458	454	526	372	528	201	480	431	197	3547
Par	4	4	4	4	5	3	4	4	3	35
Score	3	3	5	3	4	3	4	4	3	32

10	11	12	13	14	15	16	17	18	In	Total
532	391	447	194	454	161	577	458	551	3765	7312
4	4	4	3	4	3	5	4	4	37	72
5	4	4	3	4	3	5	3	4	35	67

Signature of Marker

Signature of Competitor
Darren Clarke

Noteworthy

Started at the 10th tee

- **Hole 17**: Driver, wedge, one putt from 25 feet
- **Hole 18**: Driver, 3-wood into front bunker, sand wedge, one putt from four feet
- **Hole 1**: Driver, 9-iron, one putt from eight feet
- **Hole 2**: Driver, 7-iron, one putt from 15 feet
- **Hole 3**: Three putts from 30 feet off the green
- **Hole 4**: 4-iron, 8-iron, one putt from 50 feet
- **Hole 5**: Driver, 4-iron, two putts from 60 feet

> **"** *Hoylake hasn't really bared its teeth thus far. But if it blows tomorrow, it could be a different story, because there are tough holes out there if the wind blows the way it should do.* **"**
> —Darren Clarke

Darren Clarke had a run of six birdies in seven holes starting at the 17th hole.

Fowler waits to putt at the 13th after getting within one of McIlroy with three birdies in a row.

Third Round Scores	
Players Under Par	35
Players At Par	8
Players Over Par	29

the fifth, eighth and ninth. He and Fowler were now three behind.

There was no loss of faith from McIlroy, even though it was his putter keeping him going, especially at the second, seventh and ninth holes. "Those were the most important putts for me today," he said. "Some of those par putts were even more important than the birdie or eagle putts."

McIlroy failed to make a birdie at the par-5 10th but rolled in an eight-footer at the 11th for a 3. Fowler, however, had birdied the 10th and made a 30-footer at the 11th before hitting an 8-iron to five feet at the 12th for his third in a row. When McIlroy bogeyed the same hole, missing from five feet after finding the rough off the tee, the pair were level.

"I never panicked," McIlroy said. "I didn't feel uncomfortable. My patience was rewarded today. I knew I had some holes coming up that I could take advantage of and make some birdies." First he had to get up and down from the rough at the short 13th and holed a six-footer to do so. Then came the bonus of a birdie putt from 33 feet slotting into the hole at the 14th. Fowler had bogeyed the same hole and would also take a 6 at the 16th. Now McIlroy was exactly where he wanted to be. "I felt like I was driving well, and if I could drive it on the fairway at 16 and 18, I knew I would have irons into

After dropping into a tie with Fowler, McIlroy began his stunning finish with a 20-footer for eagle at the 16th hole.

the greens for my second shots," he said. "I was sort of waiting for those holes."

At the 577-yard 16th, he hit a 4-iron from 248 yards to 20 feet and rolled in the first of his eagle efforts. Now he was five ahead. He dropped a shot at the 17th, as had Fowler and Garcia, who had birdied the 16th, but then unleashed his power again at the last. Fowler had got one last birdie there, Garcia had to settle for a 5.

"It looked like Rory might have a one- or two-shot lead, and now all of a sudden he's got a six-shot lead," Garcia said. "Rickie and I helped him a bit with that but, more than anything, he helped himself with the way he finished." Though the Spaniard rued not hitting better shots at the last two holes, he added: "Rory hit a great shot on 18. Something like that, the only thing you can do is say 'well done.'

McIlroy made his second eagle in three holes at the 18th.

Sergio Garcia plays his third shot at the 10th. He finished seven behind the leader.

> **❝ If you're disappointed at somebody making birdies and eagles, then you're not a good sportsman.**
> —Sergio Garcia ❞

"It's difficult to see anyone catching him when he's playing like that, but the only thing I can do is play well and try to put a little pressure on him and see how he reacts."

Fowler, who won his only event on the PGA Tour in a play-off over McIlroy at Quail Hollow in 2012, had similar thoughts. "I had two tee shots that got away from me on the back nine, and the approach on 17, so they cost me three shots," he said. "Playing with Rory, six back, the same position I was in today, I've got to get a good start, maybe put a little bit of pressure on him. But he's definitely in control of the golf tournament right now."

McIlroy was already being asked about being three-quarters of the way to the career Grand Slam with the prospect of victory the following day. But he just laughed it off. "It would mean a lot of hype going into Augusta next year," he said. He was not getting carried away, and invoked the way he won the BMW PGA Championship at Wentworth earlier in the season as a word of warning. "I've won from seven back this year, so I know leads can go very quickly. I'm not taking anything for granted." The Open was not won yet.

PLAYERS MOURN ESTEEMED COACH

By Alistair Tait

The third round of any golf tournament is normally called "moving day." Saturday of the 143rd Open Championship could easily have been called "Bob Torrance Day."

The esteemed coach was on the minds of most competitors as they set out for the third round. The 82-year-old Scot passed away peacefully in his sleep the previous evening at his home in Largs, Scotland, after losing a long battle with cancer. Players wore black ribbons on their golf hats as a mark of respect for one of the game's finest teachers.

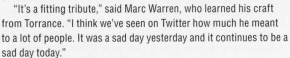

Bob Torrance (right) with Padraig Harrington and Dr Bob Rotella.

"It's a fitting tribute," said Marc Warren, who learned his craft from Torrance. "I think we've seen on Twitter how much he meant to a lot of people. It was a sad day yesterday and it continues to be a sad day today."

Torrance, along with his wife June, was a constant presence on the European Tour for more than 40 years. He made his reputation from giving his son, Sam, the swing that would earn him 21 European Tour victories, 11 European Senior Tour victories, eight Ryder Cup appearances, and a winning Ryder Cup captaincy in 2002.

Torrance was old school before the term was even coined. Sam's success persuaded many other touring pros to seek out Bob for counsel. His list of students read like a who's who of the European Tour. Major Champions Ian Woosnam, Padraig Harrington and Darren Clarke were among those who benefited from Torrance's know-how.

Stephen Gallacher

"I would not be the golfer that I am without the help of Bob Torrance," said Clarke, the 2011 Open Champion. "In 1990, I played the Irish Open and my grouping was Sam and DJ Russell. Sam told me, 'You need to turn pro sooner rather than later and you need to start working with my dad.'

"I did. And I spent many years, many days and hours with Bob, and June, working on everything. Bob was a very, very special man. He will be sadly missed. He was a character. He was difficult to understand at times, even for those of us who knew him. He was a great man. The world is a worse place without Bob Torrance."

The master coach never stopped in his search for a full understanding of the golf swing. Twice he made pilgrimages to Fort Worth, Texas, to spend time with Ben Hogan at Shady Oaks Golf Club. Torrance hit balls in front of Hogan and the two became firm friends.

When he wasn't on tour, Torrance could be found at the Inverclyde National Golf Training Centre near his Largs home. He would be there every day from 10am to 4pm, passing on his knowledge to amateurs and professionals alike, often free of charge. When asked why he did it, he simply said: "Why wouldn't I be here? This is what I love doing. I still love the game even after all these years. I'm still learning about the golf swing."

He passed that love of the game on to his players, most of whom were struggling to come to terms with his passing. Paul McGinley, the 2014 Europe Ryder Cup captain, interrupted his trip to the previous week's Scottish Open to visit the man who had coached him for more than 20 years. McGinley made the 400-mile round-trip by car from Royal Aberdeen.

"Not only was he a world-class golf coach, a fact recognised right across the game, but he was also one of my very favourite people in life," said McGinley, a four-time winner on the European Tour. "I will dearly miss his teaching and his wit."

Stephen Gallacher spoke for all when he said: "It's the end of an era. He was a character and had a lot of wisdom."

That wisdom was built on a few steadfast beliefs that Torrance never wavered from. "I've always felt that the legs are the most important muscles in the golf swing," he said. "Hogan proved that. So did Nicklaus. So has Tiger Woods. I also believe the two most important areas of the golf swing are the take-away and the start of the downswing.

"But I've always believed if something works, then don't change it. If you work on a player's strong points then you will automatically strengthen his weak points, but if you work on his weak points then you will weaken his strong points. Never weaken the strong to strengthen the weak. Why would you want to do that?"

Harrington, who won three Major Championships under Torrance's tutelage, including The Open in 2007 and 2008, called him "a father figure."

"He gave so much to the game — and we have so much in terms of his coaching, his humour, just himself that we've all gained," Harrington said. "He did this game a great service. He loved it. And whoever came into contact with him walked away better for the experience. Isn't that a fabulous way to go out of this world?"

Rory McIlroy hits a 5-iron second shot at the 18th hole for another eagle.

Round Three Hole Summary

HOLE	PAR	YARDS	EAGLES	BIRDIES	PARS	BOGEYS	D.BOGEYS	OTHER	RANK	AVERAGE
1	4	458	0	13	35	23	1	0	3	4.167
2	4	454	0	14	37	19	2	0	6	4.125
3	4	426	0	13	50	8	0	1	9	3.972
4	4	372	0	18	44	10	0	0	13	3.889
5	5	528	1	30	39	1	0	1	18	4.611
6	3	201	0	14	48	9	1	0	10	2.958
7	4	480	0	7	41	20	2	2	1	4.319
8	4	431	0	6	49	15	2	0	2	4.181
9	3	197	0	6	58	8	0	0	7	3.028
OUT	35	3,547	1	121	401	113	8	4		35.250
10	5	532	1	20	45	5	1	0	16	4.792
11	4	391	0	14	52	5	0	1	12	3.917
12	4	447	0	11	54	7	0	0	11	3.944
13	3	194	0	9	54	9	0	0	8	3.000
14	4	454	0	7	48	16	0	1	3	4.167
15	3	161	0	13	55	4	0	0	14	2.875
16	5	577	1	22	38	9	2	0	15	4.847
17	4	458	0	6	50	15	1	0	5	4.153
18	5	551	1	33	31	4	3	0	17	4.653
IN	37	3,765	3	135	427	74	7	2		36.347
TOTAL	72	7,312	4	256	828	187	15	6		71.597

Fourth Round
20 July 2014

This One's for Mum

By Andy Farrell

McIlroy holds on to win his first Open despite drama from Garcia and a late charge from Fowler.

The making of history does not come easily and no Open is won before its time. Rory McIlroy did not win the 2014 Championship on Saturday, but his stunning finish to the third round dictated how Sunday at Hoylake would play out. All he needed was to play "one more solid round" of golf. Everyone else had to provide the drama.

And so they did, with Sergio Garcia and Rickie Fowler chief among the chasers. Yet on a day when the leaderboard was littered with scores in the mid to high 60s, it was McIlroy's 71 — more than solid in the circumstances — that won the 143rd Open. That he had the odd wobble on the front nine merely led to a far more entertaining afternoon's golf than might have been expected with a player leading by six strokes at the start.

Even so, McIlroy's advantage never slipped below

McIlroy launches his celebrations for a two-stroke victory.

two shots. He was watchful, ready to unleash extra power if it were needed, but ultimately as in control as he had been all week. It was far from a procession to victory, but by the time the 25-year-old Northern Irishman reached the 18th green the acclaim for the most exciting young talent in golf more than rewarded his achievement.

Had his bunker shot at the last found the cup, as it very nearly did, pandemonium may have broken out. While two putts were required to seal victory by two strokes over Garcia and Fowler, it no longer mattered. Everyone was on their feet and McIlroy was celebrating with a hug from his mum.

It was possibly one of the loudest and most boisterous Open Sundays ever experienced and nothing could have bettered the cauldron-like atmosphere at the final hole, with its wraparound, horseshoe grandstand. All day they saluted the finishers, from the unheralded to the most illustrious, the likes of Tom Watson, Tiger Woods and Phil Mickelson. They cheered the gallant hopefuls, among them Jim Furyk and Adam Scott, who dared to dream a miracle might happen. And they rose as one to acknowledge Garcia.

4

"McIlroy is now so far ahead of the curve when it comes to European reference points that the only valid comparisons to be made are with the two Leviathans of the sport — Jack Nicklaus and Tiger Woods."

—Derek Lawrenson, *Daily Mail*

"In living a real drama of his own, Rory McIlroy has become a central character, both on and off the golf course. Compulsive, compelling, captivating: he is all of these and more."

—Philip Reid, *The Irish Times*

"Real champions can withstand real pressure and, thanks to Sergio Garcia, the tension verged on excruciating as McIlroy's six-shot lead began to tumble."

**—James Corrigan,
*The Daily Telegraph***

"On a course where Woods swatted away all before him in 2006, McIlroy provided an imperious front-running performance from the moment he signed for an opening round of 66."

—Ewan Murray, *The Guardian*

"The ship needed to be steadied. A good up-and-down from a greenside bunker at the seventh for par did the trick."

—Martin Dempster, *The Scotsman*

Starter Ivor Robson shares a joke with McIlroy and Rickie Fowler.

An 18th Open, and a 64th Major Championship, may have come and gone without the Spaniard claiming victory, but while at times he has not helped himself with his reaction to defeat on the links, on this day he was one of the heroes of Hoylake. In plain speak, he gave it a right good go. A closing 66 included a thrilling eagle at the 10th hole, but, more than the numbers, the way he treated Kipling's twin impostors just the same earned him even more affection. He returned the love by patting his chest and applauding back, saluting the fans with his cap in a 360-degree spin of the final green. "I love the 18th," he said. "That's a feeling that no one can take away from me. That's one of the reasons I love this Championship."

Finally the grand crescendo arrived as McIlroy entered the amphitheatre of dreams. For the second day running the ovation was thunderous, although this time he could enjoy it to the full. Fowler still had a putt for an eagle, which would have prolonged the tension had it dropped, but his late run of three birdies in the last four holes for a 67 at least secured him a second successive runner-up finish in a Major.

Another likeable 25-year-old, the American had again demonstrated his Major credentials, moving Mickelson to say that he was "on the brink of really doing something special." Yet when asked about

McIlroy at the first, where he matched Sergio Garcia's birdie ahead of him.

Fourth Round Leaders

HOLE	1	2	3	4	5	6	7	8	9	10	11	12	13	14	15	16	17	18	TOTAL
PAR	4	4	4	4	5	3	4	4	3	5	4	4	3	4	3	5	4	5	
Rory McIlroy	(3)	4	4	4	[6]	[4]	4	4	(2)	(4)	4	4	[4]	4	3	(4)	4	5	71-271
Sergio Garcia	(3)	4	(3)	4	(4)	3	4	4	3	(3)	4	4	3	4	[4]	(4)	4	(4)	66-273
Rickie Fowler	4	(3)	4	4	5	3	4	4	3	(4)	4	4	3	4	(2)	(4)	4	(4)	67-273
Jim Furyk	4	4	4	4	(3)	3	4	4	3	(4)	(3)	4	3	4	(2)	(4)	4	(4)	65-275
Marc Leishman	4	4	4	(3)	(4)	(2)	4	(3)	[4]	(4)	4	4	3	4	(2)	(4)	4	(4)	65-276
Adam Scott	4	(3)	(3)	4	(4)	3	[6]	4	3	(4)	(3)	4	3	(3)	3	(4)	4	(4)	66-276

TheOpen.com   TheOpen.com

> **««** *There's a lot of great venues on this rotation. This and Birkdale are my two favourites.*
>
> —Jim Furyk **»»**

It's a **Fact**

For the second year running, a player won The Open to achieve the third leg of a career Grand Slam. Phil Mickelson did so aged 43, while Rory McIlroy, at 25, became the third youngest to do so, after Jack Nicklaus, 23, and Tiger Woods, 24. Next come Gary Player, aged 26, and Byron Nelson, 28.

Fowler claimed his first birdie of the day at the second hole.

A concerned look for Garcia but the Spaniard saved par at the seventh.

his overriding memory of the week, Fowler did not hesitate in nominating the chance to share in McIlroy's march up the 18th hole. "It's definitely up there as the best walk in golf, especially Sunday when you're in the final group," he said. "To be there with Rory when he was about to win, that was fun."

McIlroy himself was finding that it takes time for such a longed-for victory to sink in. "It feels absolutely incredible," he said. One thing he noticed about the Claret Jug while parading it around the 18th green was that the engraver would not be getting a pace of play penalty. "It's sort of cool that they put your name on there even before you get it," he marvelled.

In upgrading his Silver Medal as the leading amateur from his debut at Carnoustie in 2007 to the winner's Gold Medal that accompanies the Claret Jug, McIlroy became the seventh Champion to lead outright after every round since the event was extended to 72 holes. He was the first to do so since Woods at St Andrews in 2005 but, remarkably, the second player in a row to achieve the feat at a Major, Martin Kaymer having done the same at the US Open at Pinehurst. Consecutive Major winners leading outright after each round had never happened before in the history of the game.

McIlroy also won the 2011 US Open wire-to-wire and, having claimed the US PGA Championship in 2012, now had three Major titles to his name. He was now the 16th player to have won at least three different Majors, with only Jack Nicklaus (23)

McIlroy plays from the drop zone on the right of the fifth for the first of two bogeys in a row.

❝ *The crowds were great. There was a deafening noise when you hit a good shot.* —Marc Warren **❞**

Fourth Round Scores	
Players Under Par	47
Players At Par	7
Players Over Par	18

and Woods (24) having achieved the feat at a younger age. His first chance to join those two, plus Gene Sarazen, Ben Hogan and Gary Player, in winning all four would come at the Masters in 2015.

"I'm immensely proud of myself," McIlroy said as he attempted to take it all in. "To sit here, 25 years of age, and win my third Major Championship and be three-quarters of the way to the career Grand Slam, yeah, I never dreamed of being at this point of my career so quickly.

"Especially being someone from around here, The Open Championship was the one you really wanted growing up, the one you holed so many putts on the putting green to win, to beat Tiger Woods, Sergio Garcia, Ernie Els, whatever. Didn't quite need to hole a putt today to do it, just a little tap in, which was nice."

You can tell a new generation has arrived from the names of the heroes they beat in their imagination growing up. That trio certainly experienced contrasting fortunes at Hoylake, with Garcia playing a starring role but Els missing the cut and Woods finishing in 69th place after a closing 75.

On another sunny day of benign conditions, scoring was generally far better than that, with Watson posting a 68 to head off to The Senior Open Championship at Royal Porthcawl in fine fettle. Bristol's

Fowler made par at the dangerous 14th before finishing with three birdies in the last four holes.

Low Scores

Low First Nine

Sergio Garcia	32
Marc Leishman	32
Edoardo Molinari	32
Shane Lowry	32
Robert Karlsson	32
Angel Cabrera	32

Low Second Nine

Jim Furyk	32
Adam Scott	32
Chris Wood	32

Low Round

Jim Furyk	65
Marc Leishman	65
Shane Lowry	65
Chris Wood	65

Caddie Dermot Byrne congratulates Shane Lowry on a 65.

Edoardo Molinari settles for a 68 after just missing on the 18th.

Chris Wood posted the first 65 of the day.

Jim Furyk came home in 32 helped by caddie Fluff Cowan.

Australian Marc Leishman's eagle putt at the last slipped by, so he, too, posted a 65.

Chris Wood was the first of four players to match the course record of 65, Shane Lowry also achieving that mark to finish at 10 under, alongside Graeme McDowell and Victor Dubuisson. McDowell had an extraordinary finish. After a double-bogey at the short 13th, he finished birdie-birdie-birdie-par-eagle.

Robert Karlsson showed that a charge was eminently possible with eagles at the fifth and the 10th holes, but then faltered to finish nine under. Edoardo Molinari posted a second successive 68, and his third of the week, to be 11 under with Charl Schwartzel and take the honours as the leading Italian. Scott, the world number one, who had finished second and third in the last two Opens, made three early birdies before a double-bogey at the seventh. He refused to give up, however, and five birdies coming home gave him a 66 that moved him into a tie for fifth place with his compatriot Marc Leishman, who added another 65.

Furyk returned the last 65 of the day, thanks to an eagle at the fifth and, like Scott, five birdies on the back nine. He ended up in fourth place, on 13 under, having also come fourth at Hoylake in 2006. Given that the 44-year-old American has also been fourth and

> **❝** *I stayed up late with my coach last night, until about half 11 on the sofa, chatting things through. I'd say we really got to the bottom of it and I was a different player today.*
> —Chris Wood **❞**

Championship Totals	
Rounds Under Par	168
Rounds At Par	46
Rounds Over Par	241

An erratic final round for Dustin Johnson included a detour into this bush on the fifth hole.

> **It's fun to finish with a birdie. You feel lighter. You don't feel you have a burden to take to the next tournament. Wake up in the morning not in too much pain and go from there.**
>
> —64-year-old Tom Watson

fifth at Royal Birkdale, he must like the Liverpool air.

That no one reached the 16-under-par mark at which McIlroy started the day showed how far ahead the Northern Irishman was of the field. "Yesterday's finish proved to be very important," he said. "Those two eagles went a long way in deciding this Championship. I'm happy I gave myself enough of a cushion for today, because there were a lot of guys coming at me, especially Sergio and Rickie."

Garcia and Dustin Johnson were in the penultimate pairing, and the Spaniard got off on the right foot by holing from 10 feet for a birdie. "I was excited from the moment I woke up this morning," he said. Johnson, so supreme in his 65 on Friday, would play erratically for a 72 and a tie for 12th place. Not long later, Johnson announced he was taking time away from the game to "seek professional help" for some personal challenges.

Fowler hit his approach at the first to 12 feet but first had to watch McIlroy make the perfect start by holing from 18 feet to extend his lead to seven shots. McIlroy's target for the day was to get to 20 under par, knowing if he focused on that everything else would take care

Five-time winner Tom Watson enjoyed his closing 68.

Adam Scott birdied three of the first five holes.

of itself. Fowler got back to six behind by making a 15-footer at the next, but pars to the end of the front nine were not quite what he wanted.

Garcia, however, holed a fine putt from 20 feet at the third and got up and down for a 4 at the fifth as he went out in 32 for the second day running. McIlroy had birdied the fifth on each of the first three days, but this time his 3-iron approach finished by the grandstand on the right of the hole. From deep rough in the drop zone, he pitched over the green and his chip from there did not quite get up onto the tier where the hole was positioned. He had a 12-footer for a par but missed.

His 6-iron at the short sixth ran off the left side of the green, and again he could not get down in two, missing from six feet for his par. Now McIlroy's lead was down to three strokes, and while the gallery remained wholly supportive, the

A nice way for Graeme McDowell to finish with an eagle at 18.

4

Garcia got excited with his eagle at the 10th hole.

Sergio Garcia
Inspired by Seve and a new soul mate

Sergio Garcia has had several close calls in an Open context, not least at Hoylake in 2006, only this one was different. He had given it his best shot from first until last and had never got down on himself. Quite the reverse, in fact.

"Sometimes you play well, but there is just one better player — and Rory was better," came the Spaniard's generous acknowledgement of McIlroy's victory.

Garcia was baited by a fan during the course of his closing 66, but Sunday was not a day when he was looking for excuses. At the end of the afternoon, he was more inclined to mention that he had had his share of good luck, not least after his ball had cannoned into a spectator stand at the 12th green. It reared out and dropped to the side of the putting surface to a cheerful round of applause.

Garcia was no more than two behind McIlroy after his eagle at the 10th and the same applied after the 13th. But, as he said, it had been a hard ask to make up a seven-shot deficit. "It's difficult when you know you can't make a mistake, that so much has to go right," he said. "I wanted to make Rory feel a little bit uncomfortable and see how he would respond. And he obviously responded well. Every time I got closer, he would make one more birdie."

There are girlfriends who can hold a player back, but, in Katharina Boehm, Garcia has found a genuine soul mate. Katharina graduated in Communications and Business Administration from the College of Charleston, in South Carolina, and was a member of the golf team. A former German junior international, Boehm has bonded well with the Garcia family. She and Sergio's father, Victor, regularly join forces to do battle against Sergio, and the two of them laughingly claim to have found a formula in which they usually have the beating of him.

On Thursday evening of Open week, Boehm watched the new *Seve* film with the family, an experience in which she was so moved by the sight of the Garcias all crying that she cried too. "I did not know Seve, but he was obviously a huge character and a big inspiration to Sergio," she said.

When Garcia won in Thailand at the end of 2013, Katharina, who was caddying for him, saw her main role as one of keeping Sergio's spirits up. Yet when Katharina needed a bit of consoling after Garcia had lost out to McIlroy at Hoylake, the situation was reversed. Sergio felt there was not too much to be sad about. At 34, as he said in his press conference, he has grown up a bit. "All this week has helped me," he said — and, yes, he was referring to the business of winning Majors.

One of the most oft-posed questions in golf was once, "What's wrong with Sergio?" Today, there is nothing wrong with him. As his manager says, he has maybe eight years — that is 32 chances — in which to bring home a Major. More than ever before, people believe that is going to happen.

—Lewine Mair

---

tension was beginning to build. "Five was a bad bogey, and then to follow that up with another bogey, it was a bad mistake," he said.

It was time to fall back on his two key words for the week: "process" and "spot." McIlroy explained: "With my long shots, I just wanted to stick to my process and stick to making good decisions and good swings. The process of making good swings, rather than thinking about the end result.

"And spot was for my putting. I was just picking a spot in the green and trying to roll it over my spot every time. I wasn't thinking about holing it, or what it would mean, or how many further clear it would get me. I just wanted to roll it over my spot, and if it went in, great. If it didn't, then I'd try it the next hole."

Another shot might have gone at the seventh, where his second shot finished in a bunker. His recovery to little more than a foot from the hole immediately settled the nerves. He had his par, and an 8-iron to 15 feet at the ninth set up the chance of getting back to level par for the day. He holed the putt and a huge roar went up.

In the far corner of the course, however, Garcia

A fine bunker shot at the seventh helped McIlroy to settle down after two dropped shots.

was creating his own drama. A 6-iron to 15 feet at the 10th was converted into an eagle with one strike of the putter. Now two behind, Garcia was getting excited. "Please, be good, please, please be good," he urged as his 8-iron second shot at the 11th was in the air. It wasn't quite. It stopped on the fringe, 30 feet from the hole, but Garcia thought his putt looked good. It swung with late break but just missed. "That would have been nice to see go in because I knew there were some tough holes coming up," he said.

McIlroy found the green with his second at the 10th and two-putted for his birdie to ease back to three ahead, while Fowler also got his 4. "That stretch of holes, seven, eight, nine and 10, were big for me today," McIlroy said. "Getting up and down at seven, some good shots at eight, the birdies at nine and 10 were big, especially with Sergio pushing there. I could feel a little more comfortable on the back nine."

But with the wind picking up into the players' faces on the stretch of holes along the sand dunes of the estuary, no one was that comfortable. Garcia got a helpful break when his 6-iron to the 12th green hit a railing on the grandstand on the right and bounced back into play. He had a chip from just off the green and safely got up and down, kissing the ball and lobbing it into the stand rather more gently than it had arrived from down the fairway moments earlier.

At the next hole, the short 13th, the Spaniard's 7-iron shot finished just short of the front-right bunker. Another turn of the ball and it would surely have trickled into the hazard. Perhaps he was getting all his good fortune in one go. He chipped up to a foot and tapped in for par.

Just behind, McIlroy made two pars before his 6-iron at the 13th came up surprisingly short and left of the green. From the rough he could do no more than get the ball 25 feet from the hole, from

Round of the Day: **Rory McIlroy – 71**

Noteworthy

- **Hole 1**: Driver, 8-iron from 152 yards, one putt from 18 feet
- **Hole 5**: Driver right semi-rough, 3-iron into stand right, drop zone, wedge over green, chip, two putts from 12 feet
- **Hole 6**: 6-iron left of green, chip, two putts from six feet
- **Hole 9**: 8-iron, one putt from 15 feet
- **Hole 10**: 3-wood, 5-iron from 228 yards, two putts from 24 feet
- **Hole 13**: 6-iron into left rough, pitch, two putts from 18 feet
- **Hole 16**: Driver, 7-iron from 218 yards, two putts from 45 feet

His eagle putt on the 10th missed, but a birdie still put McIlroy three ahead.

Excerpts FROM THE Press

"After all the doubts about his ability to play links golf, McIlroy is entitled to savour this success more than any other."

—**David Facey**, *The Sun*

"Boy Wonder is back. Or maybe he's just getting started again."

—**Doug Ferguson**, *Associated Press*

"Others, such as Martin Kaymer and Adam Scott, can fly, but Rory can soar."

—**Ron Green Jr**, *Global Golf Post*

"Hoylake has a habit of throwing up A-list champions and McIlroy joined a parade which includes Woods, Bobby Jones and Walter Hagen."

—**Neil Squires**, *Daily Express*

"McIlroy's three Majors have been as breathtaking as the Boy Wonder's down times in between have been befuddling."

—**Robert Lusetich**, *Fox Sports*

Fowler, whose work with Butch Harmon this year is taking hold, added another strong finish in a Major to his résumé.

—**Steve DiMeglio**, *USA Today*

"We can only imagine how loud McIlroy's inner voice was chanting to keep it all together."

—**Kevin Garside**, *The Independent*

Round Four Hole Summary

HOLE	PAR	YARDS	EAGLES	BIRDIES	PARS	BOGEYS	D.BOGEYS	OTHER	RANK	AVERAGE
1	4	458	0	5	48	17	2	0	2	4.222
2	4	454	0	12	46	14	0	0	10	4.028
3	4	426	0	7	54	8	1	2	6	4.125
4	4	372	0	20	50	2	0	0	14	3.750
5	5	528	4	42	19	5	2	0	17	4.431
6	3	201	0	5	56	10	1	0	8	3.097
7	4	480	0	10	44	13	4	1	3	4.194
8	4	431	0	19	47	6	0	0	12	3.819
9	3	197	0	12	43	15	2	0	8	3.097
OUT	35	3,547	4	132	407	90	12	3		34.764
10	5	532	5	47	18	2	0	0	18	4.236
11	4	391	0	8	55	9	0	0	11	4.014
12	4	447	0	5	51	15	1	0	4	4.167
13	3	194	0	5	55	10	2	0	6	3.125
14	4	454	0	6	45	16	4	1	1	4.292
15	3	161	0	24	40	7	1	0	13	2.792
16	5	577	3	40	23	6	0	0	16	4.444
17	4	458	0	5	51	15	1	0	4	4.167
18	5	551	2	41	21	4	4	0	15	4.542
IN	37	3,765	10	181	359	84	13	1		35.778
TOTAL	72	7,312	14	313	766	174	25	4		70.542

McIlroy chips from the rough at the 13th where a poor tee shot led to a bogey.

❝ My emotions for Rory? Envious and respectful and appreciative of the curly-haired kid.
—Graeme McDowell **❞**

❝ We used to say there would never be another Nicklaus and then along came Tiger. You never want to discount the possibility of someone coming along and dominating.
—Phil Mickelson **❞**

where he made his third bogey of the day. Garcia was now only two behind after a par at the 14th. Both McIlroy and Fowler also went on to par the 14th. The American may not have been making many birdies, but he had done well to stave off the threat of bogeys along the way.

Perhaps it was the 15th, the par 3 which turns back inland, which was decisive. Garcia put his tee shot into the bunker, pin high and to the right. By the time he got to the ball, McIlroy was watching from the tee. Did that have any effect, did Garcia even know? The crucial error was to leave his first recovery shot in the sand. He got up and down at the second attempt, but the bogey put him three behind again.

"I thought if I just got it a couple of yards over the bunker, it's going to hit a downslope and maybe I can hole it," Garcia explained. "I just got too cute. When you know you can't make any mistakes, it's hard."

McIlroy got his par at the hole and Fowler made a nice putt for a birdie. But now the leader was on safe territory, with two par 5s to come. His drive at the 16th was majestic, not least as someone who had rather too much to say at the wrong moments throughout the round had interjected during his swing. McIlroy had spotted the culprit, and the security guards ensured he had seen his last golf for the day.

Garcia hit two lovely shots down the 16th and two-putted for a birdie, but McIlroy did just the same moments later. "Once he drove it in the fairway on 16 and gave himself an easy birdie, it was going to be tough to catch him," said Fowler, who got up and down for a birdie of his own.

At the 17th, Garcia had a chance from 20 feet but missed, while McIlroy safely got his par after a delightful chip and a modest shake of the fist. All three would birdie the last, McIlroy tapping in to do so and then launching his ball high into the grandstand, where it was caught by a gentleman

A crucial moment for Garcia at the 15th, leaving his first recovery attempt (top) in the bunker.

'The one you really want' — McIlroy with the Claret Jug.

Garcia and Fowler with their runner-up salvers.

from Leeds who later put it up for auction on a golf memorabilia website.

Fred Daly had become the first Champion from Ulster at Hoylake in 1947. McIlroy became the third, following Darren Clarke in 2011, and the fourth Irishman in all including Padraig Harrington's two victories. "Rory just distanced himself from the field, especially with his finish yesterday. He was awesome," said Fowler, who became only the fourth player to record four rounds under 70 and not win. "It was a bit like the US Open for me. It's hard to be disappointed because it was such a great week."

McIlroy's 17-under-par total of 271 was just one stroke shy of the tally set by Woods at Hoylake in 2006. It was an equally dominant performance, yet followed two years of extremes. From world number one in 2012, he completely lost form in 2013, missing the cut in The Open for the first time at Muirfield. Then in 2014 he called off his planned marriage to tennis star Caroline Wozniacki, just after the wedding invitations had been sent out, but found refuge in the game of golf.

"I've really found my passion again for golf," he admitted. "Not that it ever dwindled, but it's what I think about when I get up in the morning, it's

Championship Hole Summary

HOLE	PAR	YARDS	EAGLES	BIRDIES	PARS	BOGEYS	D.BOGEYS	OTHER	RANK	AVERAGE
1	4	458	0	55	268	118	14	1	4	4.206
2	4	454	1	42	264	136	13	0	3	4.259
3	4	426	0	51	329	69	4	3	11	4.077
4	4	372	0	81	312	59	4	0	14	3.969
5	5	528	13	213	179	40	9	2	17	4.616
6	3	201	0	38	322	88	8	0	6	3.145
7	4	480	0	30	268	125	28	5	1	4.366
8	4	431	0	57	298	84	12	4	8	4.138
9	3	197	0	49	318	81	7	0	9	3.101
OUT	**35**	**3,547**	**14**	**616**	**2,558**	**800**	**99**	**15**		**35.873**
10	5	532	16	199	206	29	5	0	18	4.578
11	4	391	1	78	306	65	3	2	13	3.993
12	4	447	0	48	299	97	8	3	5	4.165
13	3	194	0	51	314	86	4	0	10	3.095
14	4	454	1	39	277	115	17	6	2	4.277
15	3	161	0	70	300	75	8	2	12	3.059
16	5	577	6	144	246	51	8	0	15	4.804
17	4	458	1	49	307	86	7	5	7	4.143
18	5	551	9	182	194	44	22	4	16	4.780
IN	**37**	**3,765**	**34**	**860**	**2,449**	**648**	**82**	**22**		**36.895**
TOTAL	**72**	**7,312**	**48**	**1,476**	**5,007**	**1,448**	**181**	**37**		**72.767**

what I think about when I go to bed. I just want to be the best golfer I can be."

Winning the BMW PGA Championship at Wentworth in May had been "huge," he said, and he is now the first player to win the two biggest British titles in the same season. "You can't doubt your own ability. The ability was still there, I was just trying to find a way to make it come out again.

"Missing the cut at Muirfield last year was a low point," he added. "I had never missed a cut in The Open before and I really missed playing on the weekend. I said to myself, I'd never let that happen again. It's been huge what a difference a year makes."

Ten years earlier, McIlroy's father, Gerry, and three friends had each put a bet of £100 at odds of 500-1 on Rory winning The Open before his 26th birthday. "It's a nice bonus for my dad, but his three friends are going to be very happy," said the new Champion Golfer of the Year.

What touched him most, however, was that his mother, Rosie, was present for the first time when he had won a Major.

"This one's for you, mum," he said.

Mum Rosie with the new Champion.

Supporters from across the Irish Sea.

INTO AN AGE OF SPLENDOUR

By John Hopkins

Rory McIlroy's victory may come to be seen as the most significant sign yet of a changing of the order of things in golf. Becoming, at 25, the third youngest man to win three different Major Championships after Jack Nicklaus and Tiger Woods moved the Northern Irishman further ahead of his contemporaries and helped to establish him as the leader of a new era.

Other sports may not be, but golf is measured in eras: The Great Triumvirate at the end of the 19th century and the start of the 20th; Walter Hagen, the flamboyant professional, and Bobby Jones, the unparalleled amateur; Ben Hogan, Byron Nelson and Sam Snead; Arnold Palmer, Jack Nicklaus and then Tom Watson; Nick Faldo leading up to Tiger Woods' time.

With a bit of luck we can say that Rory McIlroy is leading us into an Age of Edwardian Splendour after the Age of Austerity under Tiger Woods. Where Woods was stern-faced, McIlroy is smiling. Where Woods was austere, McIlroy is benevolent. Where Woods was respected, McIlroy is liked. Where Woods routed his rivals on occasion, McIlroy's victories are fewer, and, though breathtaking, are perhaps not quite so breathtaking as Woods'. Oddly, each won an Open at Hoylake by two strokes.

McIlroy talks well, plays golf beautifully. He has a normal hinterland and appears to be a thoroughly engaging young man. At his peak, Woods was a magnificent golfer whose form for a few golden years may have deserved him being described as the best golfer of all time. At all times he seemed guarded. There was a reluctance to engage with the public, a tendency to shroud his life in secrecy. He earned the respect he was given; McIlroy enjoys popularity within the game.

Acceptance speeches are often short and trite, little more than a formulaic recitation of thanks to all and sundry. McIlroy's at Hoylake was a master class of graciousness, appreciation and humour. He thanked The R&A, not just for staging The Open so well but for the work they do in other aspects of the game, an unexpected plaudit that went down a storm.

He joked about being a Manchester United supporter in a den of Liverpool supporters and got away with it. And he brought Rosie, his mother, out of the stands to acknowledge his pride in her and his gratitude to her, explaining that this was the first of his Major Championship victories that she had seen in person. Every mother in the world probably went "aaahhh" as he did so. And he paid tribute to Gerry, his father, too. In short, in doing something that is not as easy as it seems, McIlroy didn't put a foot wrong.

Later he addressed the ticklish issue of dominance in the game. "Golf is looking for someone to put their hand up, and I want to be that person," McIlroy said, without sounding boastful. "I want to be the guy that goes on to win Majors regularly. I feel like there's a lot

more left in me." He lived up to those words by winning the US PGA Championship at Valhalla the following month.

McIlroy will lead the game in a way that is unlike the way Woods did so. This is no surprise. Their personalities are as different as an Irish stew and New England clam chowder. I respect one of these two men and like the other in much the same way that years ago people respected Jack Nicklaus and liked Arnold Palmer.

Would I have dinner with Woods? Yes. Would I enjoy it? Possibly, however swift the occasion turned out to be.

Would I have dinner with McIlroy? Certainly. Would I enjoy it? Probably. JP Fitzgerald, his caddie, says he is a bit of an anorak, knowing a lot about sport. There is something easy about the way he speaks, both what he says and the way he says it.

I first saw Tiger Woods when he represented the United States in the World Amateur Team Championship — the Eisenhower Trophy — in Paris in 1994. He was 18, rake-thin and as talkative then as he was to become bland later. He said that he hadn't seen anything of Paris other than his hotel, the golf course and a local McDonald's. He also told the story of how, as a boy at school, he had suffered racial abuse when he was tied to a tree and taunted.

I first saw McIlroy as a mop-haired, round-faced 18-year-old in the 2007 Walker Cup at Royal County Down. He was a prodigy then, though less so than Woods had been at the same age. He walked and talked quickly and seemed to take no time over his putts.

McIlroy, might not, probably won't, get to Woods' current total of victories in 14 Major Championships, but he will have a broader quality of life and be more of a role model to those who come along behind him. The Age of Edwardian Splendour could be one to cherish.

McIlroy chips at the 17th hole.

The 143rd Open Championship

Complete Scores

HOLE			1	2	3	4	5	6	7	8	9	10	11	12	13	14	15	16	17	18	TOTAL
PAR	POSITION		4	4	4	4	5	3	4	4	3	5	4	4	3	4	3	5	4	5	
Rory McIlroy	1	Round 1	4	3	4	4	4	2	4	4	3	4	4	3	3	4	3	4	4	5	66
Northern Ireland	1	Round 2	5	4	4	4	4	2	4	3	3	4	4	4	3	4	2	5	3	4	66
£975,000	1	Round 3	5	4	4	4	4	3	4	4	3	5	3	5	3	3	3	3	5	3	68
	1	Round 4	3	4	4	4	6	4	4	4	2	4	4	4	4	4	3	4	4	5	71 **-271**
Sergio Garcia	T3	Round 1	3	4	3	4	4	3	4	4	3	6	3	4	2	4	3	5	4	5	68
Spain	T3	Round 2	5	2	5	4	4	3	4	4	3	4	4	4	3	5	3	5	4	4	70
£460,000	T3	Round 3	5	3	4	4	4	3	4	3	2	5	4	4	3	4	3	4	5	5	69
	T2	Round 4	3	4	3	4	4	3	4	4	3	3	4	4	3	4	4	4	4	4	66 **-273**
Rickie Fowler	T10	Round 1	4	4	4	3	4	3	4	3	3	5	4	3	3	4	4	4	5	5	69
USA	T3	Round 2	4	5	4	3	4	3	4	3	4	4	5	3	4	3	4	3	4	5	69
£460,000	2	Round 3	3	3	4	4	4	2	5	4	3	4	3	3	3	5	3	6	5	4	68
	T2	Round 4	4	3	4	4	5	3	4	4	3	4	4	4	3	4	2	4	4	4	67 **-273**
Jim Furyk	T3	Round 1	4	4	4	4	4	2	5	4	2	4	4	4	3	4	2	5	4	5	68
USA	T9	Round 2	4	5	4	4	4	3	4	4	2	5	4	4	3	4	3	4	5	5	71
£280,000	T7	Round 3	4	4	3	3	5	3	4	4	3	5	3	4	3	5	3	5	5	5	71
	4	Round 4	4	4	4	4	3	3	4	4	3	4	3	4	3	4	2	4	4	4	65 **-275**
Marc Leishman	T10	Round 1	4	4	3	4	4	3	4	4	3	4	4	5	3	4	3	5	4	4	69
Australia	T15	Round 2	4	4	4	4	5	4	4	4	4	4	4	4	2	4	4	5	4	4	72
£210,500	T12	Round 3	4	4	4	4	5	2	4	6	3	5	4	3	3	4	2	4	5	4	70
	T5	Round 4	4	4	4	3	4	2	4	3	4	4	4	4	3	4	2	4	4	4	65 **-276**
Adam Scott	T3	Round 1	4	4	4	3	3	3	4	4	2	5	4	5	2	5	3	4	4	5	68
Australia	T15	Round 2	4	5	5	4	4	3	4	4	3	5	4	5	4	4	3	5	3	4	73
£210,500	T7	Round 3	4	4	4	4	5	3	4	4	3	7	3	4	2	4	2	4	4	4	69
	T5	Round 4	4	3	3	4	4	3	6	4	3	4	3	4	3	3	4	4	4	4	66 **-276**
Charl Schwartzel	T33	Round 1	4	3	4	5	4	5	4	4	3	5	4	4	3	5	3	4	3	4	71
South Africa	T3	Round 2	3	4	4	4	4	3	4	5	2	4	3	4	3	6	3	4	3	4	67
£154,250	T7	Round 3	4	4	4	3	4	2	5	4	3	6	4	4	4	3	3	5	5	5	72
	T7	Round 4	4	4	4	4	4	3	4	4	3	4	5	4	3	4	2	4	4	4	67 **-277**
Edoardo Molinari	T3	Round 1	3	3	4	4	5	3	4	4	3	4	4	5	3	4	3	4	4	4	68
Italy	T15	Round 2	4	4	4	5	5	3	4	5	3	6	4	3	2	3	3	5	4	6	73
£154,250	6	Round 3	3	3	4	4	5	3	5	4	3	4	4	3	4	4	2	5	4	4	68
	T7	Round 4	4	4	4	4	4	4	3	3	2	5	4	4	3	4	3	5	4	4	68 **-277**

*Denotes amateur

HOLE			1	2	3	4	5	6	7	8	9	10	11	12	13	14	15	16	17	18	
PAR	POSITION		4	4	4	4	5	3	4	4	3	5	4	4	3	4	3	5	4	5	TOTAL
Shane Lowry	T3	Round 1	5	3	4	4	5	3	5	4	3	4	3	3	3	3	3	5	4	4	68
Republic of Ireland	T24	Round 2	4	4	4	5	4	3	6	6	4	5	3	4	3	4	3	5	4	4	75
£112,667	T23	Round 3	4	3	3	4	4	2	4	4	3	5	5	5	3	3	3	5	5	5	70
	T9	Round 4	4	3	4	4	4	3	4	4	2	4	4	4	3	4	2	4	4	4	65 -278
Graeme McDowell	T84	Round 1	4	5	3	4	4	3	4	4	3	7	4	4	4	4	4	3	5	5	74
Northern Ireland	T24	Round 2	3	5	4	4	4	4	4	4	4	4	3	4	3	3	3	5	4	4	69
£112,667	T12	Round 3	4	5	4	4	5	2	4	5	3	4	4	3	4	3	2	5	4	4	68
	T9	Round 4	4	5	4	4	4	3	3	4	3	4	4	4	5	3	2	4	4	3	67 -278
Victor Duibuisson	T84	Round 1	4	5	5	4	4	3	4	4	4	5	4	3	5	3	5	5	5	4	74
France	T12	Round 2	4	3	4	3	5	3	4	4	4	4	3	4	3	4	4	4	3	4	66
£112,667	5	Round 3	4	5	3	4	4	2	3	4	3	5	4	3	4	3	5	4	4	4	68
	T9	Round 4	5	4	4	3	3	3	4	4	3	5	4	4	4	4	4	4	4	4	70 -278
Ryan Moore	T19	Round 1	4	4	3	4	5	2	4	4	3	5	4	4	3	4	3	5	4	5	70
USA	T3	Round 2	4	5	4	4	5	3	5	3	2	4	4	4	2	4	3	5	3	4	68
£84,667	T12	Round 3	5	4	4	4	5	3	6	4	4	5	4	3	3	4	3	4	4	4	73
	T12	Round 4	4	4	4	4	4	3	3	5	3	5	5	4	3	3	2	3	4	5	68 -279
Robert Karlsson	T10	Round 1	4	4	4	4	5	4	4	4	3	4	4	3	3	4	2	4	4	5	69
Sweden	T12	Round 2	4	4	4	3	5	5	4	4	3	4	4	4	3	4	3	5	4	4	71
£84,667	T7	Round 3	4	4	3	4	4	3	4	4	3	5	4	4	3	5	2	6	4	4	70
	T12	Round 4	4	3	4	3	3	3	4	5	3	3	4	6	3	4	3	6	4	4	69 -279
Dustin Johnson	T33	Round 1	4	3	4	4	5	3	4	4	3	5	4	5	3	3	3	5	4	5	71
USA	2	Round 2	3	4	3	4	4	3	4	4	3	4	3	4	3	4	3	5	3	4	65
£84,667	T3	Round 3	3	4	4	4	5	3	5	5	4	5	4	4	2	4	2	5	4	4	71
	T12	Round 4	4	4	4	4	6	3	4	4	3	4	4	3	3	4	2	4	5	7	72 -279
Francesco Molinari	T3	Round 1	5	4	4	4	4	3	4	4	2	5	3	4	3	5	3	4	4	3	68
Italy	T3	Round 2	5	3	3	4	4	3	4	6	4	4	4	4	2	3	3	5	4	5	70
£68,667	T23	Round 3	5	5	5	4	5	3	5	4	3	5	4	5	3	4	3	4	4	4	75
	T15	Round 4	4	3	4	4	4	3	4	4	3	4	4	4	3	4	3	5	4	3	67 -280
David Howell	T49	Round 1	5	4	3	3	4	3	6	4	3	4	4	4	3	4	3	5	4	5	72
England	T19	Round 2	4	5	4	4	4	4	4	4	4	5	4	3	3	4	3	4	3	4	70
£68,667	T19	Round 3	4	5	4	3	4	3	4	4	3	4	4	4	3	4	4	5	4	4	70
	T15	Round 4	4	4	4	3	6	3	3	4	2	4	4	5	3	4	2	4	4	5	68 -280
Stephen Gallacher	T19	Round 1	4	4	4	3	4	2	4	4	4	4	4	4	4	4	3	5	5	4	70
Scotland	T19	Round 2	3	4	4	4	4	3	5	4	4	5	4	4	3	4	4	4	4	5	72
£68,667	T19	Round 3	4	5	3	4	4	3	3	4	3	6	4	3	3	4	3	5	4	5	70
	T15	Round 4	4	4	4	4	4	3	4	4	3	4	5	4	3	3	3	4	3	5	68 -280
George Coetzee	T19	Round 1	4	5	3	4	6	3	4	4	2	5	3	4	3	4	3	5	3	5	70
South Africa	T9	Round 2	4	5	4	4	4	3	4	4	3	4	4	4	2	3	2	6	5	4	69
£61,500	T23	Round 3	5	4	4	4	5	3	4	4	3	5	4	4	3	5	2	6	4	5	74
	18	Round 4	3	4	4	4	4	3	5	4	3	4	4	4	3	5	2	4	4	4	68 -281
Angel Cabrera	T124	Round 1	4	5	6	5	4	3	4	5	3	5	4	4	3	4	4	4	5	4	76
Argentina	T43	Round 2	4	4	4	3	4	3	5	4	3	3	4	4	3	5	3	5	4	4	69
£55,000	T34	Round 3	3	4	3	4	5	3	5	5	3	4	3	4	3	4	3	5	4	5	70
	T19	Round 4	4	4	4	3	4	3	4	3	3	4	4	4	3	4	2	4	5	5	67 -282
Keegan Bradley	T66	Round 1	4	5	4	4	4	3	4	4	3	5	3	5	4	4	3	5	4	5	73
USA	T31	Round 2	3	4	4	3	5	4	6	4	3	4	3	5	3	4	2	4	5	5	71
£55,000	T23	Round 3	4	4	4	3	5	2	5	4	3	5	4	4	3	4	2	4	4	5	69
	T19	Round 4	4	4	5	3	4	3	3	4	3	4	4	4	3	5	3	5	4	4	69 -282

HOLE			1	2	3	4	5	6	7	8	9	10	11	12	13	14	15	16	17	18	
PAR	POSITION		4	4	4	4	5	3	4	4	3	5	4	4	3	4	3	5	4	5	TOTAL
Chris Kirk	T33	Round 1	4	4	3	4	5	4	4	4	3	4	4	4	3	4	3	4	5	5	71
USA	T43	Round 2	5	4	3	6	4	3	4	4	4	5	4	4	3	5	3	5	4	4	74
£55,000	T23	Round 3	4	4	4	4	5	4	3	3	3	5	3	4	3	4	3	5	3	4	68
	T19	Round 4	4	4	4	4	5	3	4	4	3	4	4	3	3	4	3	4	4	5	69 -282
Matteo Manassero	2	Round 1	3	4	3	4	5	3	4	4	4	4	3	5	3	4	2	4	4	4	67
Italy	T19	Round 2	4	5	4	3	4	4	4	5	3	5	5	4	3	6	3	5	4	4	75
£55,000	T7	Round 3	5	5	3	3	4	2	5	4	3	5	4	4	3	3	3	5	3	4	68
	T19	Round 4	4	4	4	4	5	4	4	4	3	4	4	4	3	6	3	4	4	4	72 -282
Chris Wood	T105	Round 1	3	5	4	4	5	3	5	4	2	7	4	4	3	4	4	5	4	5	75
England	T43	Round 2	3	5	4	4	5	3	3	5	3	4	4	5	3	4	3	4	4	4	70
£46,167	T52	Round 3	3	5	4	3	5	3	5	5	4	5	4	4	3	4	2	5	4	5	73
	T23	Round 4	4	4	4	3	5	3	4	3	3	4	4	4	3	4	2	4	3	4	65 -283
Phil Mickelson	T84	Round 1	4	4	4	4	5	3	5	4	2	4	4	4	4	5	3	5	4	6	74
USA	T31	Round 2	4	4	5	3	3	3	4	5	3	5	4	4	3	4	3	5	4	4	70
£46,167	T34	Round 3	3	5	4	4	5	4	5	4	4	4	4	3	2	4	3	5	4	5	71
	T23	Round 4	4	4	4	3	4	3	5	4	3	4	4	4	3	4	4	4	4	4	68 -283
Justin Rose	T49	Round 1	4	4	4	4	4	4	4	3	3	4	4	5	3	5	3	5	4	5	72
England	T19	Round 2	4	4	4	4	5	3	5	4	2	3	4	4	3	5	3	5	4	4	70
£46,167	T12	Round 3	4	4	3	4	4	4	4	4	3	5	4	4	3	4	3	5	3	4	69
	T23	Round 4	4	4	4	3	5	3	4	3	3	4	4	5	5	5	3	4	4	5	72 -283
Thomas Bjørn	T19	Round 1	4	4	4	4	5	3	4	3	3	5	4	4	3	4	3	4	4	5	70
Denmark	T15	Round 2	3	4	5	4	4	3	5	5	3	5	3	4	3	4	3	4	4	5	71
£38,250	T45	Round 3	5	5	4	4	4	3	5	5	3	5	4	4	3	4	3	4	4	7	76
	T26	Round 4	4	4	4	3	4	3	4	3	4	4	4	4	3	4	2	5	4	4	67 -284
Ben Martin	T33	Round 1	5	4	5	4	4	3	4	4	2	4	4	4	2	4	3	5	4	6	71
USA	T31	Round 2	5	4	4	4	4	3	5	4	3	5	3	4	3	6	2	4	4	6	73
£38,250	T31	Round 3	4	4	4	3	5	3	4	4	3	5	4	3	3	4	3	5	4	4	70
	T26	Round 4	4	4	4	4	4	3	4	4	3	4	3	5	4	4	3	4	5	4	70 -284
Brian Harman	T49	Round 1	4	5	5	4	3	4	5	4	2	3	3	4	4	5	4	4	4	5	72
USA	T43	Round 2	5	4	5	3	4	3	4	5	3	5	3	5	4	4	3	4	4	5	73
£38,250	T23	Round 3	4	3	4	3	5	3	3	4	3	5	4	3	3	4	3	5	4	5	68
	T26	Round 4	5	5	7	3	4	3	4	4	2	3	4	4	3	4	3	4	4	5	71 -284
Byeong-Hun An	T49	Round 1	3	4	4	4	5	3	6	4	3	4	5	4	3	4	4	4	4	4	72
Korea	T24	Round 2	4	5	4	4	5	3	4	4	3	4	4	4	3	4	3	4	4	5	71
£38,250	T19	Round 3	3	4	3	4	4	2	4	4	4	4	4	4	3	5	3	5	4	5	69
	T26	Round 4	4	5	4	4	4	4	4	4	3	5	4	4	3	4	3	4	5	4	72 -284
Jimmy Walker	T10	Round 1	4	4	4	3	6	2	4	4	3	5	5	4	3	4	2	4	3	5	69
USA	T12	Round 2	5	5	5	4	4	2	6	4	3	4	4	3	2	4	3	4	4	5	71
£38,250	T12	Round 3	4	3	3	4	4	3	5	4	3	5	4	4	4	4	3	5	4	5	71
	T26	Round 4	4	5	3	3	4	3	5	4	4	4	4	4	3	7	3	5	4	4	73 -284
Darren Clarke	T49	Round 1	5	4	3	4	7	3	5	4	3	4	3	3	4	3	4	5	4	4	72
Northern Ireland	T31	Round 2	3	4	5	3	4	3	4	4	3	5	4	5	3	5	4	5	4	4	72
£38,250	T12	Round 3	3	3	5	3	4	3	4	4	3	5	4	4	3	4	3	5	3	4	67
	T26	Round 4	4	5	4	4	4	3	4	4	3	5	4	5	3	2	6	4	4		73 -284
DA Points	T105	Round 1	4	4	5	4	5	3	5	4	4	4	4	4	3	5	3	5	4	5	75
USA	T31	Round 2	4	5	4	4	5	3	4	3	3	4	4	4	3	3	3	5	3	5	69
£31,000	T38	Round 3	5	4	4	4	5	4	4	4	3	5	3	4	3	4	3	5	4	4	72
	T32	Round 4	5	3	4	3	4	3	5	4	3	4	3	5	3	4	3	4	4	5	69 -285

HOLE			1	2	3	4	5	6	7	8	9	10	11	12	13	14	15	16	17	18	
PAR	POSITION		4	4	4	4	5	3	4	4	3	5	4	4	3	4	3	5	4	5	TOTAL
Hunter Mahan	T33	Round 1	4	4	5	4	5	3	4	4	4	4	4	4	2	3	4	4	4	5	71
USA	T31	Round 2	4	5	4	5	4	3	4	3	3	5	3	4	4	4	4	5	4	5	73
£31,000	T38	Round 3	3	5	4	4	5	3	4	4	4	5	4	4	4	4	3	5	3	4	72
	T32	Round 4	4	4	4	3	5	3	4	4	3	4	4	4	3	4	2	6	4	4	69 -285
David Hearn	T19	Round 1	4	4	4	4	4	3	4	3	3	5	4	5	3	4	2	5	4	5	70
Canada	T24	Round 2	4	4	4	3	5	4	5	4	4	6	4	4	3	4	3	5	3	4	73
£31,000	T31	Round 3	4	4	4	4	5	2	4	5	3	4	4	4	3	4	3	5	4	4	71
	T32	Round 4	4	5	4	3	4	3	5	4	3	4	5	5	3	4	3	4	4	4	71 -285
Kristoffer Broberg	T19	Round 1	3	4	4	4	5	3	5	4	2	5	4	4	3	4	3	5	4	4	70
Sweden	T24	Round 2	5	3	4	5	4	3	4	4	4	5	4	4	2	4	3	5	4	6	73
£31,000	T23	Round 3	4	4	4	3	5	3	4	4	4	5	4	4	2	5	3	5	4	4	70
	T32	Round 4	4	4	4	4	4	3	4	4	4	5	3	4	4	4	2	5	4	6	72 -285
Louis Oosthuizen	T19	Round 1	3	4	4	4	5	2	4	4	3	4	4	5	3	4	3	6	4	4	70
South Africa	T3	Round 2	3	4	4	4	4	3	4	4	4	4	4	3	4	3	3	5	5	4	68
£27,083	T31	Round 3	5	5	4	4	5	3	3	3	4	5	4	4	3	5	3	6	6	4	76
	T36	Round 4	5	4	4	5	4	3	4	4	3	5	4	4	3	4	3	5	3	5	72 -286
Jordan Spieth	T33	Round 1	4	4	3	3	6	4	4	4	3	4	4	4	3	4	3	4	5	5	71
USA	T56	Round 2	4	5	5	4	4	3	4	4	3	6	3	4	4	5	3	5	4	5	75
£27,083	T23	Round 3	3	4	3	5	4	3	4	4	3	4	3	4	3	4	3	4	4	5	67
	T36	Round 4	4	4	4	4	4	3	5	4	3	5	3	5	3	6	3	4	4	5	73 -286
Branden Grace	T33	Round 1	4	5	3	5	2	5	3	3	4	4	4	4	3	4	3	6	4	5	71
South Africa	T24	Round 2	5	5	4	4	4	4	3	3	3	4	4	5	3	4	3	5	4	5	72
£27,083	T19	Round 3	3	5	4	5	4	3	4	5	2	4	4	4	3	4	2	4	4	5	69
	T36	Round 4	4	4	5	4	4	4	5	3	4	6	5	5	3	3	3	4	4	4	74 -286
Brendon Todd	T66	Round 1	4	4	4	4	4	3	4	4	2	5	4	7	3	4	4	4	4	5	73
USA	T56	Round 2	4	4	4	5	4	4	4	4	3	4	3	4	4	4	3	6	4	5	73
£21,219	T63	Round 3	5	4	5	3	5	3	4	5	2	5	4	4	3	4	2	5	5	6	74
	T39	Round 4	4	5	4	4	4	3	4	3	3	4	4	4	3	3	3	3	4	5	67 -287
Koumei Oda	T10	Round 1	5	5	4	4	4	3	4	4	3	4	4	4	3	3	2	5	3	5	69
Japan	T56	Round 2	4	5	4	4	5	3	4	5	3	6	5	4	3	5	3	5	4	5	77
£21,219	T63	Round 3	5	5	4	5	4	3	4	4	3	4	4	4	3	4	3	6	5	4	74
	T39	Round 4	4	3	7	4	4	2	3	3	3	5	4	3	3	4	3	4	3	5	67 -287
Henrik Stenson	T49	Round 1	5	4	4	4	4	3	4	4	3	4	3	6	3	4	3	5	5	4	72
Sweden	T43	Round 2	4	5	4	4	4	4	3	4	3	4	5	5	4	5	2	5	4	4	73
£21,219	T52	Round 3	4	4	4	3	4	3	3	6	3	4	4	4	3	5	4	7	4	4	73
	T39	Round 4	4	4	4	4	4	3	4	3	3	4	4	4	3	4	3	4	5	5	69 -287
Hideki Matsuyama	T10	Round 1	4	4	3	4	4	3	3	4	3	5	4	5	4	3	4	4	4	4	69
Japan	T24	Round 2	3	5	4	4	4	3	4	4	3	4	4	5	3	4	4	5	5	6	74
£21,219	T38	Round 3	5	4	4	4	5	4	4	4	3	5	5	3	2	4	3	5	5	4	73
	T39	Round 4	5	4	4	4	4	4	4	3	2	4	5	4	4	4	3	5	4	4	71 -287
Gary Woodland	T105	Round 1	5	5	5	3	4	3	5	4	3	4	4	4	3	4	3	5	4	7	75
USA	T31	Round 2	4	4	4	4	3	2	4	5	3	5	4	4	3	4	3	5	4	4	69
£21,219	T38	Round 3	4	4	4	4	5	4	4	4	3	4	4	4	3	4	3	5	4	5	72
	T39	Round 4	4	4	4	4	4	3	4	4	4	4	4	4	3	5	3	4	4	5	71 -287
Thongchai Jaidee	T49	Round 1	4	4	4	4	6	3	4	4	3	5	4	3	3	4	3	5	4	5	72
Thailand	T31	Round 2	3	4	4	3	4	3	5	5	2	5	3	5	3	5	3	6	4	5	72
£21,219	T38	Round 3	5	6	4	4	5	3	5	3	3	4	3	4	3	4	3	5	4	4	72
	T39	Round 4	4	4	4	4	5	4	3	4	2	5	5	4	2	4	2	6	5	4	71 -287

HOLE			1	2	3	4	5	6	7	8	9	10	11	12	13	14	15	16	17	18	
PAR	POSITION		4	4	4	4	5	3	4	4	3	5	4	4	3	4	3	5	4	5	TOTAL
Kevin Stadler	T66	Round 1	4	5	5	4	3	3	4	6	3	5	3	3	3	4	3	4	6	5	73
USA	T43	Round 2	4	4	4	4	4	3	5	4	2	6	3	4	2	6	3	5	4	5	72
£21,219	T38	Round 3	4	3	4	4	5	4	4	3	3	5	4	5	4	4	3	4	4	4	71
	T39	Round 4	4	4	3	4	6	2	3	4	4	4	4	5	4	5	2	5	4	4	71 -287
Marc Warren	T33	Round 1	3	4	3	4	4	4	4	4	3	4	4	5	2	5	3	6	4	5	71
Scotland	T9	Round 2	4	3	4	4	4	4	4	5	3	5	3	3	3	3	3	5	4	4	68
£21,219	T12	Round 3	4	5	4	3	4	3	4	5	4	5	3	4	3	4	3	5	4	5	72
	T39	Round 4	6	4	3	4	5	3	5	4	4	4	4	4	3	5	3	5	5	5	76 -287
Stewart Cink	T33	Round 1	4	5	5	4	4	3	4	3	3	4	4	4	3	4	3	5	5	4	71
USA	T56	Round 2	5	6	4	4	5	4	6	4	3	4	3	4	3	4	3	4	4	5	75
£16,013	T58	Round 3	4	4	4	5	5	3	4	4	2	5	4	4	3	5	3	5	4	5	73
	T47	Round 4	5	4	5	4	3	3	4	3	3	4	4	4	3	6	4	3	3	4	69 -288
Grégory Bourdy	T105	Round 1	5	6	3	4	5	3	6	4	3	4	4	3	3	4	4	5	4	5	75
France	T31	Round 2	4	4	4	5	3	4	4	3	5	4	3	3	4	3	5	4	3	4	69
£16,013	T52	Round 3	6	5	3	3	4	4	4	4	3	5	4	3	3	4	3	6	4	6	74
	T47	Round 4	5	4	3	4	4	3	4	4	3	4	4	4	2	5	3	5	4	5	70 -288
Paul Casey	T84	Round 1	4	5	4	5	5	2	4	4	3	5	4	4	3	4	4	5	4	5	74
England	T43	Round 2	4	5	4	4	4	4	4	4	3	4	4	4	4	4	3	4	4	4	71
£16,013	T52	Round 3	4	3	5	4	3	3	7	4	3	3	4	4	3	7	3	4	4	5	73
	T47	Round 4	4	4	5	3	4	3	4	4	4	4	4	4	3	4	3	5	4	4	70 -288
Zach Johnson	T33	Round 1	4	4	4	4	5	3	4	3	3	4	5	3	4	4	4	5	4	4	71
USA	T56	Round 2	5	5	4	4	5	3	5	4	4	4	4	4	3	4	3	6	4	4	75
£16,013	T45	Round 3	4	4	4	5	5	3	3	5	3	5	3	4	3	4	3	4	4	5	71
	T47	Round 4	4	4	5	4	4	3	3	3	4	5	4	4	3	4	3	4	5	5	71 -288
Tom Watson	T66	Round 1	3	5	4	4	4	3	5	6	3	5	3	4	3	4	2	5	5	5	73
USA	T56	Round 2	3	4	4	4	3	5	4	4	6	4	4	3	5	3	3	5	4	5	73
£14,650	T68	Round 3	5	4	4	4	4	3	4	4	3	4	4	4	3	5	2	7	5	6	75
	T51	Round 4	5	3	4	4	4	3	3	4	3	5	4	4	3	4	3	4	4	4	68 -289
Jason Dufner	T19	Round 1	4	4	4	3	5	3	4	4	2	5	4	4	3	4	3	5	3	6	70
USA	T31	Round 2	4	5	4	5	5	3	4	4	4	4	4	5	3	3	3	4	5	5	74
£14,650	T52	Round 3	5	4	4	4	5	3	5	5	3	5	4	4	3	4	4	4	4	4	74
	T51	Round 4	4	5	4	4	5	3	4	3	2	3	5	4	3	5	3	6	4	4	71 -289
Bill Haas	T19	Round 1	4	4	5	4	4	3	4	5	3	4	3	3	3	4	3	5	4	5	70
USA	T19	Round 2	4	4	4	5	4	2	5	4	3	5	4	4	3	4	3	6	4	4	72
£14,650	T34	Round 3	4	5	4	4	4	3	5	5	3	6	4	4	2	4	2	4	5	5	73
	T51	Round 4	6	4	4	4	5	3	4	4	3	4	4	4	3	5	3	5	5	4	74 -289
Matt Kuchar	T66	Round 1	5	5	3	4	5	3	6	3	3	4	4	3	4	5	4	5	4	3	73
USA	T31	Round 2	4	4	4	4	6	3	4	4	3	4	4	4	2	4	3	4	5	5	71
£13,925	T52	Round 3	4	5	5	5	5	3	4	5	3	4	4	4	3	3	3	5	4	5	74
	T54	Round 4	4	3	4	4	4	3	4	5	2	5	4	4	3	4	3	6	4	6	72 -290
Matt Jones	T33	Round 1	4	6	6	4	5	3	4	3	3	4	3	3	3	4	3	5	5	3	71
Australia	T43	Round 2	4	4	4	4	5	3	5	4	3	4	4	5	3	5	3	5	4	5	74
£13,925	T45	Round 3	5	3	4	3	4	2	4	4	3	5	5	4	3	4	3	4	5	7	72
	T54	Round 4	4	4	5	4	4	3	5	5	3	4	4	4	4	4	2	4	4	6	73 -290
Kevin Na	T124	Round 1	5	4	4	4	5	3	5	5	3	4	4	4	4	4	5	5	4	4	76
USA	T56	Round 2	4	4	4	4	4	4	4	4	3	4	3	4	3	4	3	5	4	5	70
£13,925	T38	Round 3	4	4	5	4	4	3	4	4	3	5	4	3	2	4	3	5	5	4	70
	T54	Round 4	5	4	4	4	6	2	6	4	3	4	4	3	2	4	3	5	4	7	74 -290

		HOLE	1	2	3	4	5	6	7	8	9	10	11	12	13	14	15	16	17	18	
	POSITION	PAR	4	4	4	4	5	3	4	4	3	5	4	4	3	4	3	5	4	5	TOTAL
Kevin Streelman	T49	Round 1	4	4	4	4	5	3	4	4	2	5	4	4	3	4	4	4	5	5	72
USA	T56	Round 2	4	5	4	5	4	4	4	4	3	4	4	4	3	4	4	5	4	5	74
£13,925	T34	Round 3	4	3	5	4	5	3	4	4	3	4	4	4	2	4	3	4	5	4	69
	T54	Round 4	4	4	3	4	5	3	4	4	3	4	4	4	3	6	3	5	5	7	75 **-290**
Ryan Palmer	T84	Round 1	4	4	4	4	5	4	4	4	2	5	4	5	4	5	3	5	4	4	74
USA	T43	Round 2	5	4	4	4	4	3	3	5	4	5	4	4	3	4	3	5	3	4	71
£13,350	T68	Round 3	5	3	4	4	5	3	5	4	3	6	5	4	3	5	3	5	4	5	76
	T58	Round 4	5	3	4	4	5	3	4	4	3	5	4	4	3	4	3	4	4	4	70 **-291**
Jamie McCleary	T66	Round 1	5	4	4	4	4	3	4	4	3	5	5	5	3	5	2	5	3	5	73
Scotland	T56	Round 2	4	5	4	4	5	3	4	4	3	5	3	4	3	3	3	6	4	6	73
£13,350	T68	Round 3	4	3	4	3	8	3	4	4	3	5	4	4	3	4	3	5	4	7	75
	T58	Round 4	4	3	4	3	5	5	4	3	3	3	3	5	3	4	5	5	4	4	70 **-291**
John Senden	T33	Round 1	4	5	4	4	4	3	4	4	3	4	4	3	3	4	3	5	5	5	71
Australia	T43	Round 2	4	5	4	4	4	3	5	6	2	4	4	4	4	4	3	6	3	5	74
£13,350	T63	Round 3	5	4	5	5	5	3	5	4	3	4	4	4	3	4	3	6	4	4	75
	T58	Round 4	5	4	4	4	5	2	4	4	4	4	4	4	4	4	2	5	4	4	71 **-291**
Jason Day	T66	Round 1	5	4	4	4	4	3	5	4	2	5	5	5	2	4	3	5	4	5	73
Australia	T56	Round 2	4	4	4	3	5	3	5	4	3	5	4	4	4	5	3	5	4	4	73
£13,350	T63	Round 3	4	5	4	5	4	3	4	4	3	4	4	4	4	5	3	5	4	5	74
	T58	Round 4	4	4	4	3	5	3	4	5	3	4	4	4	3	5	4	4	4	4	71 **-291**
Chris Rodgers	T66	Round 1	5	4	4	4	5	3	4	4	3	5	5	5	3	4	2	5	4	5	73
England	T31	Round 2	5	4	4	4	5	4	4	3	2	4	4	5	3	3	3	5	4	5	71
£13,350	T45	Round 3	5	4	4	4	6	2	4	4	3	5	4	4	4	3	5	3	5	3	73
	T58	Round 4	4	4	5	3	4	3	6	4	3	4	4	4	4	4	3	5	5	5	74 **-291**
Brandt Snedeker	T84	Round 1	5	5	4	4	5	3	4	4	2	4	4	6	2	3	4	5	5	5	74
USA	T56	Round 2	3	4	4	4	6	3	5	4	3	4	4	4	3	5	3	5	4	4	72
£13,350	T45	Round 3	4	4	4	4	4	2	4	5	3	5	4	5	2	5	3	4	4	5	71
	T58	Round 4	5	4	4	4	4	3	4	4	5	5	3	4	3	4	4	5	5	4	74 **-291**
Billy Hurley III	T66	Round 1	4	5	4	5	4	2	5	4	4	5	5	4	3	3	2	5	5	4	73
USA	T43	Round 2	4	4	4	4	6	3	5	4	3	5	4	4	3	4	3	4	3	5	72
£12,900	T68	Round 3	4	4	7	4	4	3	4	4	4	5	4	4	3	5	3	6	4	4	76
	T64	Round 4	5	5	4	4	5	3	5	4	2	4	5	3	2	4	3	5	4	4	71 **-292**
Thorbjørn Olesen	T105	Round 1	5	4	5	3	5	3	4	4	3	4	5	3	5	3	5	4	5	6	75
Denmark	T56	Round 2	4	3	4	4	4	3	3	4	3	5	4	4	4	4	3	6	4	5	71
£12,900	T58	Round 3	5	4	3	4	5	3	5	4	3	5	4	4	4	5	3	4	4	4	73
	T64	Round 4	5	5	4	4	4	3	5	3	4	4	4	4	3	5	2	4	6	4	73 **-292**
Luke Donald	T66	Round 1	5	4	4	4	4	3	4	4	3	4	4	5	3	4	4	5	4	4	73
England	T56	Round 2	4	5	4	4	4	3	4	4	3	5	5	4	5	2	5	4	5	4	73
£12,900	T45	Round 3	4	4	4	5	5	2	6	4	3	5	4	4	3	3	3	4	4	4	71
	T64	Round 4	4	5	4	4	4	3	5	4	4	4	4	5	4	5	2	5	5	4	75 **-292**
Charley Hoffman	T84	Round 1	4	3	4	4	6	3	4	3	3	5	4	5	3	4	4	5	5	5	74
USA	T56	Round 2	4	5	4	4	4	4	4	5	3	4	3	4	3	4	3	5	5	4	72
£12,650	72	Round 3	5	3	4	5	5	5	4	5	3	5	4	4	3	4	3	5	4	5	76
	T67	Round 4	3	3	4	3	7	4	5	5	2	4	4	4	3	5	2	4	4	5	71 **-293**
Brooks Koepka	T3	Round 1	3	6	4	3	4	2	4	4	3	5	4	4	2	5	3	4	4	4	68
USA	T43	Round 2	5	3	4	4	4	3	5	5	4	3	3	4	4	4	6	6	4	6	77
£12,650	T58	Round 3	4	4	4	3	5	3	4	4	3	5	7	5	3	4	3	4	4	5	74
	T67	Round 4	4	4	4	4	4	3	4	3	5	5	4	5	3	4	4	4	4	6	74 **-293**

HOLE			1	2	3	4	5	6	7	8	9	10	11	12	13	14	15	16	17	18	
PAR	POSITION		4	4	4	4	5	3	4	4	3	5	4	4	3	4	3	5	4	5	TOTAL
Tiger Woods	T10	Round 1	5	5	4	4	4	3	4	4	3	5	3	3	2	5	2	4	4	5	69
USA	T56	Round 2	6	5	4	4	5	3	4	4	3	5	4	4	3	4	3	5	7	4	77
£12,500	T58	Round 3	3	6	4	4	5	3	7	4	2	4	3	4	3	4	4	4	4	5	73
	69	Round 4	3	5	4	4	5	3	6	4	2	5	5	5	3	5	3	4	4	5	75 -294
Martin Kaymer	T66	Round 1	4	4	3	4	7	3	5	3	3	4	4	4	3	5	3	5	4	5	73
Germany	T43	Round 2	3	3	4	4	4	3	6	5	4	5	4	4	3	5	3	4	4	4	72
£12,400	T45	Round 3	5	4	4	4	4	3	5	3	2	4	4	4	3	5	3	5	4	6	72
	70	Round 4	5	5	6	5	5	4	4	3	4	5	4	4	3	4	2	5	4	7	79 -296
Matt Every	T105	Round 1	4	4	4	4	5	4	5	6	3	4	4	4	3	4	2	4	4	7	75
USA	T56	Round 2	4	4	4	4	4	4	4	4	3	5	4	5	2	4	3	5	4	4	71
£12,300	T58	Round 3	5	4	4	4	5	3	4	4	3	5	4	3	3	4	3	6	4	5	73
	71	Round 4	5	5	4	4	7	3	4	3	4	4	4	5	3	5	3	5	5	5	78 -297
Rhein Gibson	T49	Round 1	4	4	3	4	6	4	5	5	3	4	4	4	2	4	3	5	3	5	72
Australia	T56	Round 2	4	4	4	5	5	3	6	4	3	4	3	4	3	6	3	5	4	4	74
£12,200	T63	Round 3	3	5	4	3	4	4	5	4	3	6	4	5	3	4	4	4	4	5	74
	72	Round 4	5	4	5	4	5	4	7	4	3	6	4	5	2	4	4	4	4	4	78 -298

NON QUALIFIERS AFTER 36 HOLES

(Leading 10 professionals and ties receive £3,800 each, next 20 professionals and ties receive £3,100 each, remainder of professionals receive £2,600 each.)

HOLE			1	2	3	4	5	6	7	8	9	10	11	12	13	14	15	16	17	18	
PAR	POSITION		4	4	4	4	5	3	4	4	3	5	4	4	3	4	3	5	4	5	TOTAL
Hiroshi Iwata	T19	Round 1	4	6	3	4	5	3	4	4	3	4	3	4	3	4	2	5	4	5	70
Japan	**T73**	Round 2	5	5	3	3	4	4	4	5	3	3	5	5	3	4	3	5	6	7	77 -147
Nick Watney	T49	Round 1	4	4	4	4	5	5	5	4	4	5	5	4	2	4	2	3	4	4	72
USA	**T73**	Round 2	4	4	4	4	5	3	5	4	4	4	4	4	4	4	4	5	4	5	75 -147
Shawn Stefani	T66	Round 1	5	4	3	3	5	3	4	4	3	5	5	4	3	4	3	5	4	6	73
USA	**T73**	Round 2	5	4	4	4	4	3	5	5	2	5	4	4	3	4	4	5	5	4	74 -147
Graham DeLaet	T33	Round 1	4	4	4	4	3	4	3	3	5	5	5	3	4	4	4	4	4	4	71
Canada	**T73**	Round 2	6	5	4	4	4	3	4	7	5	4	4	4	3	4	3	3	4	5	76 -147
Lee Westwood	T33	Round 1	4	4	4	3	4	3	5	3	4	4	4	5	3	4	3	5	4	5	71
England	**T73**	Round 2	4	5	4	5	5	3	4	6	3	5	3	4	3	5	3	5	4	5	76 -147
Rafael Cabrera-Bello	T19	Round 1	5	5	4	4	4	3	4	4	3	4	4	4	3	3	3	5	4	4	70
Spain	**T73**	Round 2	3	4	4	4	6	4	4	4	3	7	3	4	3	4	4	5	4	7	77 -147
Oliver Fisher	T49	Round 1	4	5	3	4	5	3	4	4	2	5	4	4	3	4	3	4	4	7	72
England	**T73**	Round 2	5	4	5	4	4	3	5	4	3	5	4	4	3	4	3	5	4	6	75 -147
Dawie van der Walt	T33	Round 1	4	5	4	4	3	3	3	4	3	5	5	5	3	4	3	5	4	4	71
South Africa	**T73**	Round 2	4	5	4	4	6	3	4	5	3	5	4	4	3	4	4	6	3	5	76 -147
Kiradech Aphibarnrat	T49	Round 1	4	4	3	4	4	3	6	4	5	5	4	4	2	4	3	4	4	5	72
Thailand	**T73**	Round 2	5	4	5	4	4	3	4	3	4	6	4	3	3	5	4	5	4	5	75 -147
Ashley Chesters*	T19	Round 1	3	4	5	4	4	3	5	4	4	5	3	3	3	4	4	4	4	4	70
England	**T73**	Round 2	4	5	5	4	6	4	5	5	3	5	4	4	3	5	2	5	3	5	77 -147
Justin Leonard	T84	Round 1	4	6	4	3	5	3	4	4	3	5	4	4	3	5	3	5	4	5	74
USA	**T73**	Round 2	5	4	4	4	5	4	5	4	3	6	4	4	2	4	3	4	4	4	73 -147
KJ Choi	T49	Round 1	3	4	4	3	5	3	4	4	4	4	5	5	2	5	2	4	5	6	72
Korea	**T73**	Round 2	4	4	4	5	5	3	4	3	4	4	5	4	3	5	3	5	5	5	75 -147

	POSITION	Round	1	2	3	4	5	6	7	8	9	10	11	12	13	14	15	16	17	18	TOTAL
PAR			4	4	4	4	5	3	4	4	3	5	4	4	3	4	3	5	4	5	
Ian Poulter England	T66	Round 1	4	5	5	4	6	3	4	5	3	3	3	4	3	5	3	5	4	4	73
	T73	Round 2	4	4	4	4	4	3	4	4	5	5	4	4	4	4	4	4	5	4	74-**147**
Paul McKechnie Scotand	T124	Round 1	5	4	4	4	5	3	4	5	3	4	3	4	3	6	3	5	5	6	76
	T73	Round 2	4	4	4	4	4	3	6	4	3	4	4	5	3	4	2	4	4	5	71-**147**
Oscar Floren Sweden	T66	Round 1	5	4	4	4	5	3	4	4	3	5	4	4	4	4	3	5	3	5	73
	T73	Round 2	4	4	4	4	4	3	5	4	4	4	5	4	3	3	5	5	4	5	74-**147**
Yoshinobu Tsukada Japan	T10	Round 1	5	4	4	3	4	3	4	4	3	5	4	4	2	3	4	4	4	5	69
	T73	Round 2	4	4	4	4	6	3	5	4	3	4	4	6	3	5	3	5	5	6	78-**147**
Brendon de Jonge Zimbabwe	T140	Round 1	4	5	4	4	5	3	5	5	3	5	5	6	2	5	3	4	4	6	78
	T89	Round 2	4	5	3	4	4	4	5	4	3	3	3	4	4	4	3	5	4	4	70-**148**
Cheng-tsung Pan* Taiwan	T84	Round 1	4	4	4	5	5	3	6	4	3	5	3	4	3	3	4	5	4	5	74
	T89	Round 2	3	4	4	6	4	4	4	5	3	4	5	4	4	4	2	5	4	5	74-**148**
Boo Weekley USA	T10	Round 1	4	4	4	3	4	3	4	4	2	5	4	4	3	5	3	5	3	5	69
	T89	Round 2	4	5	5	4	5	3	4	4	4	6	4	4	4	5	4	5	4	5	79-**148**
Danny Willett England	T84	Round 1	5	5	4	4	5	3	4	5	3	5	4	4	3	5	2	5	4	4	74
	T89	Round 2	5	4	4	4	4	3	5	5	3	5	4	5	3	4	3	5	3	5	74-**148**
Miguel Á Jiménez Spain	T105	Round 1	4	4	4	3	5	4	4	4	3	5	4	6	3	5	3	5	4	5	75
	T89	Round 2	3	4	5	5	4	3	4	7	3	5	4	4	3	4	3	4	3	5	73-**148**
Bubba Watson USA	T124	Round 1	4	4	4	3	4	3	4	4	4	5	7	5	4	4	3	4	4	6	76
	T89	Round 2	3	4	4	4	4	4	4	4	3	4	3	5	3	5	4	4	4	6	72-**148**
Billy Horschel USA	T66	Round 1	4	4	5	4	7	3	4	4	3	4	4	4	4	4	3	4	4	4	73
	T89	Round 2	4	4	4	4	6	4	5	6	3	5	4	4	3	4	3	5	4	3	75-**148**
Ryo Ishikawa Japan	T84	Round 1	4	5	4	4	4	3	5	4	3	5	4	4	3	4	3	7	4	4	74
	T89	Round 2	4	6	4	4	6	4	4	5	3	4	5	3	3	3	3	5	3	5	74-**148**
John Daly USA	T134	Round 1	5	5	5	4	4	3	4	5	3	4	4	4	3	5	4	5	4	6	77
	T89	Round 2	4	5	4	4	4	3	5	5	4	5	4	4	2	4	2	5	3	4	71-**148**
Ross Fisher England	T84	Round 1	5	4	4	4	4	4	4	5	3	5	4	4	3	4	5	4	4	4	74
	T89	Round 2	4	4	4	5	4	4	5	4	3	4	4	4	4	5	3	4	5	4	74-**148**
Paul Dunne* Republic of Ireland	T105	Round 1	5	4	4	4	4	3	4	5	3	4	4	4	4	4	5	5	4	6	75
	T89	Round 2	6	5	5	5	4	3	5	4	3	5	4	4	2	3	2	4	4	5	73-**148**
Cameron Tringale USA	T84	Round 1	4	4	5	5	5	3	4	4	3	4	4	4	3	4	4	5	5	4	74
	T89	Round 2	6	5	4	4	5	4	4	4	3	5	4	4	3	4	2	5	3	5	74-**148**
Erik Compton USA	T33	Round 1	5	5	4	3	4	3	5	3	3	4	3	4	4	4	3	4	5	5	71
	T89	Round 2	4	5	4	4	7	3	4	4	3	5	4	4	3	4	6	5	3	5	77-**148**
Hyung-Sung Kim Korea	T49	Round 1	5	4	4	4	4	4	4	4	3	4	3	4	2	6	3	5	4	5	72
	T89	Round 2	4	4	4	5	5	4	4	5	3	5	4	4	4	4	4	5	3	5	76-**148**
Freddie Jacobson Sweden	T19	Round 1	3	4	4	5	5	3	4	4	3	5	4	4	3	4	3	4	4	4	70
	T89	Round 2	4	4	5	4	5	3	4	6	4	4	4	4	4	6	3	5	4	5	78-**148**
Ben Curtis USA	T84	Round 1	5	4	4	4	3	5	4	2	4	4	4	4	3	4	3	5	5	7	74
	T89	Round 2	4	4	4	5	6	3	4	3	3	5	6	3	3	5	3	5	4	4	74-**148**
Mikko Ilonen Finland	T19	Round 1	4	4	4	4	6	2	3	4	4	4	4	4	3	4	3	5	4	5	70
	T89	Round 2	5	5	5	4	5	4	5	4	3	4	5	5	2	4	4	5	4	5	78-**148**
Harris English USA	T49	Round 1	3	5	4	4	5	3	4	4	3	4	5	4	3	5	3	4	4	5	72
	T89	Round 2	4	4	4	5	5	4	5	4	3	4	4	4	3	4	3	5	5	6	76-**148**
Brett Rumford Australia	T105	Round 1	4	4	4	3	5	4	5	3	4	5	4	5	3	6	3	4	4	5	75
	T89	Round 2	4	4	4	5	4	3	6	5	3	3	4	4	3	4	3	5	5	4	73-**148**
John Singleton England	T140	Round 1	4	4	4	4	5	3	4	4	4	4	6	4	5	3	6	5	5	5	78
	T89	Round 2	4	4	4	4	5	4	4	4	3	4	4	4	3	5	2	4	4	4	70-**148**

	POSITION		1	2	3	4	5	6	7	8	9	10	11	12	13	14	15	16	17	18	TOTAL
PAR			4	4	4	4	5	3	4	4	3	5	4	4	3	4	3	5	4	5	
Hyung-Tae Kim	T105	Round 1	5	4	4	4	6	4	4	4	3	4	4	5	3	4	4	5	4	4	75
Korea	**T89**	Round 2	4	4	4	4	4	3	5	4	4	5	4	4	3	4	3	5	4	5	73 -**148**
Scott Stallings	T105	Round 1	5	4	5	4	6	2	5	5	3	5	5	4	3	4	3	6	2	4	75
USA	**T110**	Round 2	4	5	3	4	5	3	3	4	4	5	3	3	3	5	4	7	4	5	74 -**149**
Yusaku Miyazato	T49	Round 1	5	4	4	5	4	3	4	4	2	3	5	4	4	4	4	5	4	4	72
Japan	**T110**	Round 2	4	4	4	3	5	4	5	4	3	6	3	4	5	4	4	6	5	4	77 -**149**
George McNeill	T124	Round 1	5	5	4	4	5	3	4	4	3	5	5	5	2	5	3	6	4	4	76
USA	**T110**	Round 2	4	4	3	3	5	3	4	5	4	6	4	4	4	5	3	4	4	4	73 -**149**
Rhys Enoch	T66	Round 1	4	4	5	4	4	3	6	4	2	4	5	3	3	5	3	5	4	5	73
Wales	**T110**	Round 2	5	4	4	5	5	3	4	4	4	5	2	7	3	4	3	6	3	5	76 -**149**
Patrick Reed	T140	Round 1	4	4	4	4	5	3	3	5	3	5	5	4	3	5	3	5	5	8	78
USA	**T110**	Round 2	4	5	4	4	6	4	4	4	3	5	3	3	3	4	3	4	4	4	71 -**149**
Juvic Pagunsan	T124	Round 1	6	4	4	4	6	3	3	5	3	4	5	4	4	4	3	4	5	5	76
Philippines	**T110**	Round 2	4	3	4	6	5	3	5	4	3	4	4	4	4	5	2	5	4	4	73 -**149**
Jonas Blixt	T105	Round 1	4	5	4	4	5	3	4	4	3	4	5	4	3	6	4	5	4	5	75
Sweden	**T116**	Round 2	4	3	4	4	5	3	4	5	4	5	4	4	3	4	4	5	4	6	75 -**150**
G Fdez-Castaño	T84	Round 1	3	4	4	4	4	3	6	4	3	4	4	5	4	5	3	4	4	6	74
Spain	**T116**	Round 2	4	4	4	5	6	3	4	4	3	5	5	4	4	5	3	5	4	4	76 -**150**
Tommy Fleetwood	T84	Round 1	4	4	4	4	4	3	4	5	4	4	4	5	3	4	3	6	4	5	74
England	**T116**	Round 2	5	4	3	4	5	3	5	4	4	6	4	5	4	4	3	4	4	5	76 -**150**
Matthew Baldwin	T124	Round 1	5	4	4	4	4	3	4	4	3	5	4	5	3	4	4	5	4	7	76
England	**T116**	Round 2	5	5	4	4	4	3	4	3	3	5	5	4	4	4	3	5	4	5	74 -**150**
Anirban Lahiri	T105	Round 1	4	4	4	5	4	3	6	5	2	4	4	4	3	4	4	5	5	5	75
India	**T116**	Round 2	4	4	5	4	6	3	3	4	5	5	4	4	3	4	3	6	4	4	75 -**150**
Victor Riu	T84	Round 1	6	4	4	4	5	3	5	4	3	5	4	4	2	5	3	4	4	5	74
France	**T121**	Round 2	4	4	4	4	5	4	4	5	4	5	4	5	3	5	3	6	3	6	77 -**151**
YE Yang	T105	Round 1	5	4	4	4	4	3	4	4	4	5	5	4	4	4	3	5	4	5	75
Korea	**T121**	Round 2	4	5	4	4	6	3	4	4	3	6	3	5	4	4	3	5	3	6	76 -**151**
Ashun Wu	T105	Round 1	4	4	4	4	5	4	5	4	2	6	5	4	3	4	3	6	4	4	75
China	**T121**	Round 2	4	4	4	4	6	4	5	4	4	4	5	4	3	5	2	5	4	5	76 -**151**
JB Holmes	T84	Round 1	3	4	4	4	4	3	5	4	3	5	5	4	4	4	5	4	4	5	74
USA	**T121**	Round 2	4	4	4	4	5	3	4	3	3	6	4	5	4	4	3	5	8	4	77 -**151**
Jamie Donaldson	T145	Round 1	4	4	5	5	4	3	5	5	4	5	4	5	3	6	3	5	4	5	79
Wales	**T121**	Round 2	5	4	4	3	5	3	3	4	3	4	4	4	3	5	4	4	4	6	72 -**151**
Chesson Hadley	T145	Round 1	5	5	4	5	4	4	5	4	3	6	4	4	4	4	3	5	4	6	79
USA	**T121**	Round 2	5	4	4	4	5	3	4	3	3	6	4	4	3	5	3	5	3	4	72 -**151**
Justin Walters	T134	Round 1	4	5	5	4	4	4	4	4	3	5	4	4	4	4	3	7	5	4	77
South Africa	**T121**	Round 2	4	4	3	4	4	4	4	4	3	5	4	5	3	4	5	5	4	5	74 -**151**
M Kobayashi	T140	Round 1	4	6	4	6	5	3	4	4	4	4	4	2	4	3	4	5	8		78
Japan	**T121**	Round 2	3	5	5	4	5	3	5	5	3	5	5	3	3	2	3	5	4	5	73 -**151**
Bernd Wiesberger	T49	Round 1	6	4	5	4	4	3	4	3	3	5	3	4	3	4	4	4	4	4	72
Austria	**T121**	Round 2	6	4	5	4	5	3	4	5	3	5	5	4	4	4	4	5	4	5	79 -**151**
Todd Hamilton	T134	Round 1	5	4	4	4	6	3	5	3	3	5	4	6	4	5	3	5	4	4	77
USA	**T121**	Round 2	3	5	4	4	6	3	4	4	3	4	5	4	4	4	3	5	5	4	74 -**151**
Tyrrell Hatton	T105	Round 1	5	4	3	3	8	3	4	4	4	5	5	4	3	5	3	5	4	3	75
England	**T131**	Round 2	5	5	5	4	4	3	5	4	3	5	5	3	3	3	4	6	5	5	77 -**152**
Pablo Larrazábal	T105	Round 1	5	4	4	5	5	3	5	4	3	4	4	4	2	6	3	5	5	4	75
Spain	**T131**	Round 2	4	4	6	4	5	4	4	4	3	5	4	4	4	4	3	4	5	6	77 -**152**

	POSITION		1	2	3	4	5	6	7	8	9	10	11	12	13	14	15	16	17	18	TOTAL
PAR			4	4	4	4	5	3	4	4	3	5	4	4	3	4	3	5	4	5	
Ernie Els	T145	Round 1	7	5	4	5	5	4	5	4	3	5	4	5	3	4	3	4	4	5	79
South Africa	**T131**	Round 2	4	4	4	4	7	3	4	4	3	5	3	5	3	4	3	5	4	4	73 -152
Richard Sterne	T66	Round 1	4	5	4	3	5	3	5	4	3	4	4	4	4	4	3	6	4	4	73
South Africa	**T131**	Round 2	5	5	4	4	4	3	5	5	4	5	5	5	4	4	4	6	3	4	79 -152
David Duval	T66	Round 1	4	4	5	4	5	3	4	5	3	5	3	4	3	4	3	6	4	4	73
USA	**T131**	Round 2	4	4	5	5	6	4	4	5	3	4	5	4	4	4	3	5	5	5	79 -152
Padraig Harrington	T84	Round 1	4	4	4	4	4	4	5	4	3	5	4	4	3	4	3	6	5	4	74
Republic of Ireland	**T131**	Round 2	4	5	4	5	5	4	4	4	3	5	4	4	3	5	4	5	4	6	78 -152
Webb Simpson	T124	Round 1	4	5	4	4	5	3	4	3	4	5	4	5	4	5	3	5	4	5	76
USA	**T137**	Round 2	4	4	4	4	4	3	5	5	4	6	3	4	3	4	2	7	4	7	77 -153
Sir Nick Faldo	T124	Round 1	4	4	4	4	5	3	5	4	3	5	4	4	3	6	2	5	5	6	76
England	**T137**	Round 2	4	5	4	4	5	3	5	4	3	5	5	4	3	5	3	5	4	6	77 -153
Tomohiro Kondo	T124	Round 1	4	5	4	4	4	4	4	4	3	4	4	4	4	5	3	4	7	5	76
Japan	**T137**	Round 2	4	5	4	5	5	3	5	4	3	5	5	4	3	3	4	6	4	5	77 -153
Brendan Steele	T84	Round 1	6	6	4	3	6	4	4	4	3	4	3	4	3	4	3	5	3	5	74
USA	**T140**	Round 2	5	6	5	4	4	3	4	5	4	4	4	5	3	5	3	5	4	7	80 -154
Scott Jamieson	T134	Round 1	4	5	4	3	6	2	5	4	3	5	5	4	4	5	4	6	4	4	77
Scotland	**T140**	Round 2	5	5	5	5	3	4	8	5	3	5	4	3	3	4	2	5	4	4	77 -154
Paul Lawrie	T145	Round 1	4	5	4	4	5	3	5	4	4	6	3	5	3	5	3	5	6	5	79
Scotland	**T140**	Round 2	6	4	5	4	4	3	4	4	4	5	3	4	3	4	3	5	4	6	75 -154
Roberto Castro	T84	Round 1	4	5	4	4	5	2	4	4	3	6	5	3	3	4	3	6	4	5	74
USA	**T143**	Round 2	4	5	5	5	4	5	4	5	3	4	5	4	3	4	4	6	5	6	81 -155
Russell Henley	T105	Round 1	4	5	4	3	4	3	4	3	3	4	4	5	5	4	3	5	4	8	75
USA	**T143**	Round 2	4	5	4	4	4	5	4	7	4	5	4	5	3	5	3	5	4	5	80 -155
Jin Jeong	T134	Round 1	5	5	4	4	4	3	5	5	3	5	4	5	3	4	3	5	4	6	77
Korea	**T143**	Round 2	3	5	4	4	5	3	4	7	3	5	4	5	2	5	3	5	6	5	78 -155
Bradley Neil*	T145	Round 1	5	5	4	4	7	3	4	5	4	5	3	5	3	5	3	4	4	5	79
Scotland	**T143**	Round 2	4	4	5	4	6	3	4	5	3	4	4	4	3	7	4	5	3	4	76 -155
Christopher Hanson	T153	Round 1	4	5	4	6	5	2	7	4	3	4	5	5	3	4	4	4	4	8	81
England	**T143**	Round 2	4	4	4	4	6	3	5	5	3	4	4	5	3	4	3	5	4	4	74 -155
Matthew Southgate	152	Round 1	4	4	4	4	4	3	6	4	3	4	4	5	3	5	5	6	7	5	80
England	**T148**	Round 2	4	4	4	5	4	3	6	4	4	4	4	4	4	3	3	6	4	6	76 -156
Chris Stroud	T145	Round 1	5	4	4	4	7	3	4	4	3	4	5	5	4	5	3	5	5	5	79
USA	**T148**	Round 2	4	5	4	5	5	3	5	4	3	4	4	3	4	4	3	5	5	7	77 -156
Peter Uihlein	T134	Round 1	5	4	5	5	5	4	6	4	3	4	4	4	3	7	3	4	4	3	77
USA	**T148**	Round 2	4	6	4	5	4	4	5	3	3	5	5	4	3	4	3	6	4	7	79 -156
Dong-Kyu Jang	T140	Round 1	4	4	4	3	6	3	4	4	3	4	5	4	4	5	5	5	6	5	78
Korea	**T151**	Round 2	4	5	4	4	5	3	4	4	4	5	4	5	4	5	4	7	4	4	79 -157
Joost Luiten	T153	Round 1	4	5	4	4	5	5	5	6	3	5	4	4	3	4	3	5	5	7	81
Netherlands	**T151**	Round 2	4	4	4	5	5	4	4	5	4	3	4	4	3	4	4	4	4	7	76 -157
Mark Wiebe	T145	Round 1	5	4	4	4	4	4	5	4	3	5	5	5	4	5	4	5	4	5	79
USA	**T151**	Round 2	4	4	4	4	4	3	5	5	5	5	4	4	3	5	3	5	4	7	78 -157
Sandy Lyle	155	Round 1	4	3	4	5	4	4	6	5	3	4	6	5	2	7	4	6	4	6	82
Scotland	**154**	Round 2	6	5	4	5	5	3	5	4	3	5	4	3	4	5	3	6	7	7	84 -166
Bryden Macpherson	156	Round 1	5	4	5	4	5	4	6	5	3	7	6	8	4	7	3	5	4	5	90
Australia	**155**	Round 2	5	5	5	5	5	3	4	5	4	4	4	4	3	5	3	7	4	5	80 -170
Michael Hoey	T105	Round 1	4	4	4	4	4	3	5	4	3	6	3	4	4	5	4	5	4	5	75
Northern Ireland	**156**	Round 1	5	4	5	4	5	4	4												**WD**

THE TOP TENS

Driving Distance

1. *Rory McIlroy* *327.8*
2. Brooks Koepka 327.5
3. Adam Scott 315.4
4. Dustin Johnson 310.3
5. Angel Cabrera 304.1
6. Keegan Bradley 301.9
7. Paul Casey 300.6
8. Justin Rose 299.0
9. Hunter Mahan 298.0
10. Darren Clarke 296.8

Fairways Hit
Maximum of 56

1. **Chris Rodgers** **44**
2. Jim Furyk 43
3. Kristoffer Broberg 41
3. Henrik Stenson 41
5. Adam Scott 40
5. Ryan Moore 40
5. Francesco Molinari 40
5. Ben Martin 40
9. 7 players tied 39
20. *Rory McIlroy* *37*

Greens in Regulation
Maximum of 72

1. **Adam Scott** **57**
2. Ryan Moore 55
3. David Howell 54
3. Kristoffer Broberg 54
3. Paul Casey 54
6. Phil Mickelson 53
6. Byeong-Hun An 53
6. Hunter Mahan 53
9. Marc Leishman 52
9. Shane Lowry 52
9. Jason Dufner 52
25. *Rory McIlroy* *49*

Putts

1. **Matteo Manassero** **107**
2. Jim Furyk 108
2. Koumei Oda 108
4. *Rory McIlroy* *110*
4. Sergio Garcia 110
4. Stephen Gallacher 110
4. Marc Warren 110
8. Edoardo Molinari 111
8. Francesco Molinari 111
8. Chris Wood 111
8. Brandt Snedeker 111

McIlroy savours the moment in front of the world's press photographers.

Statistical Rankings

	Driving Distance	Rank	Fairways Hit	Rank	Greens In Regulation	Rank	Putts	Rank
Byeong-Hun An	280.5	38	39	9	53	6	123	61
Thomas Bjørn	283.8	33	35	36	51	12	119	46
Grégory Bourdy	262.9	70	34	43	46	46	117	36
Keegan Bradley	301.9	6	36	28	50	16	120	55
Kristoffer Broberg	288.9	20	41	3	54	3	124	67
Angel Cabrera	304.1	5	33	47	49	25	117	36
Paul Casey	300.6	7	32	53	54	3	124	67
Stewart Cink	292.1	14	28	65	45	53	116	29
Darren Clarke	296.8	10	35	36	46	46	117	36
George Coetzee	271.3	63	30	59	47	40	114	20
Jason Day	291.1	18	33	47	43	59	116	29
Luke Donald	272.3	57	29	62	39	70	115	24
Victor Dubuisson	279.6	40	34	43	49	25	116	29
Jason Dufner	272.3	57	33	47	52	9	126	71
Matt Every	291.1	18	26	70	46	46	129	72
Rickie Fowler	281.6	36	36	28	51	12	112	12
Jim Furyk	285.9	26	43	2	48	32	108	2
Stephen Gallacher	278.6	43	31	56	44	56	110	4
Sergio Garcia	294.0	11	38	16	51	12	110	4
Rhein Gibson	286.8	23	26	70	39	70	117	36
Branden Grace	286.6	24	30	59	43	59	112	12
Bill Haas	269.1	67	35	36	50	16	123	61
Brian Harman	293.6	12	34	43	43	59	112	12
David Hearn	263.3	69	39	9	50	16	120	55
Charley Hoffman	285.0	29	28	65	43	59	117	36
David Howell	252.4	72	38	16	54	3	119	46
Billy Hurley III	259.5	71	37	20	46	46	119	46
Thongchai Jaidee	277.6	46	37	20	44	56	113	15
Dustin Johnson	310.3	4	32	53	50	16	114	20
Zach Johnson	284.3	31	37	20	49	25	122	59
Matt Jones	284.1	32	31	56	45	53	114	20
Robert Karlsson	280.4	39	36	28	50	16	113	15
Martin Kaymer	285.8	27	23	72	47	40	124	67
Chris Kirk	279.0	41	34	43	49	25	115	24
Brooks Koepka	327.5	2	29	62	42	64	118	41
Matt Kuchar	274.3	54	35	36	47	40	119	46
Marc Leishman	286.9	22	33	47	52	9	113	15
Shane Lowry	272.6	56	36	28	52	9	115	24
Hunter Mahan	298.0	9	37	20	53	6	125	70
Matteo Manassero	273.3	55	30	59	43	59	107	1
Ben Martin	292.1	14	40	5	48	32	116	29
Hideki Matsuyama	272.0	59	39	9	44	56	118	41
Graeme McDowell	274.4	52	39	9	48	32	113	15
Rory McIlroy	327.8	1	37	20	49	25	110	4
Jamie McLeary	271.1	64	37	20	46	46	115	24
Phil Mickelson	284.5	30	36	28	53	6	118	41
Edoardo Molinari	271.4	62	33	47	48	32	111	8
Francesco Molinari	275.3	50	40	5	46	46	111	8
Ryan Moore	270.0	66	40	5	55	2	120	55
Kevin Na	283.1	34	39	9	42	64	114	20
Koumei Oda	275.4	48	36	28	40	68	108	2
Thorbjørn Olesen	278.1	45	39	9	42	64	119	46
Louis Oosthuizen	283.0	35	29	62	50	16	123	61
Ryan Palmer	293.6	12	28	65	47	40	123	61
DA Points	278.5	44	37	20	51	12	120	55
Chris Rodgers	268.3	68	44	1	49	25	123	61
Justin Rose	299.0	8	38	16	50	16	119	46
Charl Schwartzel	287.6	21	35	36	50	16	115	24
Adam Scott	315.4	3	40	5	57	1	118	41
John Senden	275.1	51	35	36	38	72	113	15
Brandt Snedeker	281.6	37	28	65	40	68	111	8
Jordan Spieth	277.1	47	32	53	45	53	116	29
Kevin Stadler	274.3	53	28	65	50	16	122	59
Henrik Stenson	291.6	17	41	3	48	32	119	46
Kevin Streelman	275.3	49	38	16	48	32	119	46
Brendon Todd	286.6	25	39	9	47	40	116	29
Jimmy Walker	271.5	61	35	36	49	25	116	29
Marc Warren	270.9	65	31	56	42	64	110	4
Tom Watson	271.9	60	36	28	47	40	118	41
Chris Wood	278.9	42	36	28	46	46	111	8
Gary Woodland	285.6	28	33	47	48	32	123	61
Tiger Woods	292.1	14	37	20	48	32	119	46

	Driving Distance	Rank	Fairways Hit	Rank	Greens In Regulation	Rank	Putts	Rank
Kiradech Aphibarnrat	279.8	76	17	61	21	76	58	49
Matthew Baldwin	263.3	137	19	21	21	76	63	134
Jonas Blixt	289.5	43	17	61	20	92	62	123
Rafael Cabrera-Bello	284.5	58	14	115	22	59	59	67
Roberto Castro	269.8	123	16	81	10	155	56	17
Ashley Chesters*	283.5	60	15	99	23	44	61	110
KJ Choi	290.3	40	15	99	22	59	60	88
Erik Compton	284.5	58	14	115	21	76	58	49
Ben Curtis	288.8	46	21	6	21	76	60	88
John Daly	306.5	12	9	154	14	149	54	6
Brendon de Jonge	292.0	36	16	81	21	76	58	49
Graham DeLaet	303.0	18	18	37	22	59	60	88
Jamie Donaldson	267.3	129	13	129	17	133	57	31
Paul Dunne*	266.5	132	16	81	16	142	55	8
David Duval	253.0	150	13	129	20	92	64	142
Ernie Els	292.0	36	15	99	22	59	66	151
Harris English	300.3	20	16	81	27	5	68	155
Rhys Enoch	287.8	48	17	61	20	92	59	67
Sir Nick Faldo	258.0	146	19	21	18	122	61	110
Gonzalo Fdez-Castaño	298.5	23	17	61	17	133	58	49
Oliver Fisher	279.5	78	19	21	19	113	57	31
Ross Fisher	289.8	41	18	37	24	30	66	151
Tommy Fleetwood	283.0	64	18	37	20	92	62	123
Oscar Floren	287.8	48	12	138	18	122	56	17
Chesson Hadley	283.5	60	13	129	14	149	56	17
Todd Hamilton	277.0	89	19	21	20	92	61	110
Christopher Hanson	303.5	17	15	99	21	76	62	123
Padraig Harrington	288.5	47	12	138	14	149	57	31
Tyrrell Hatton	263.3	137	17	61	17	133	58	49
Russell Henley	306.3	13	11	148	15	144	60	88
JB Holmes	275.8	97	15	99	18	122	58	49
Billy Horschel	275.8	97	19	21	22	59	63	134
Mikko Ilonen	283.5	60	17	61	23	44	58	49
Ryo Ishikawa	274.3	106	15	99	21	76	59	67
Hiroshi Iwata	262.8	142	19	21	20	92	55	8
Freddie Jacobson	293.3	33	17	61	18	122	58	49
Scott Jamieson	269.3	126	13	129	18	122	60	88
Dong-Kyu Jang	276.5	93	21	6	15	144	62	123
Jin Jeong	274.0	109	12	138	19	113	60	88
Miguel Ángel Jiménez	276.5	93	20	15	23	44	59	67
Hyung-Sung Kim	266.8	130	12	138	18	122	56	17
Hyung-Tae Kim	289.5	43	18	37	17	133	57	31
Masanori Kobayashi	270.0	122	12	138	18	122	57	31
Tomohiro Kondo	272.8	113	14	115	20	92	63	134
Anirban Lahiri	279.3	80	16	81	19	113	59	67
Pablo Larrazábal	281.5	69	12	138	17	133	59	67
Paul Lawrie	282.5	66	16	81	18	122	62	123
Justin Leonard	250.8	155	17	61	24	30	62	123
Joost Luiten	289.8	41	19	21	18	122	63	134
Sandy Lyle	280.7	71	11	148	13	152	65	148
Bryden Macpherson	255.0	149	12	138	12	154	62	123
Paul McKechnie	273.0	112	17	61	21	76	58	49
George McNeill	272.0	117	18	37	22	59	62	123
Yusaku Miyazato	266.8	130	16	81	23	44	66	151
Bradley Neil*	282.0	67	13	129	17	133	62	123
Juvic Pagunsan	289.5	43	11	148	16	142	57	31
Cheng-tsung Pan*	252.0	153	14	115	20	92	56	17
Ian Poulter	286.0	55	21	6	22	59	61	110
Patrick Reed	278.8	81	13	129	19	113	57	31
Victor Riu	269.3	126	19	21	20	92	59	67
Brett Rumford	278.8	81	16	81	17	133	55	8
Webb Simpson	275.3	100	18	37	15	144	58	49
John Singleton	279.8	76	10	152	15	144	55	8
Matthew Southgate	277.8	86	12	138	17	133	60	88
Scott Stallings	280.0	74	15	99	20	92	58	49
Brendan Steele	287.3	51	16	81	20	92	62	123
Shawn Stefani	275.8	97	20	15	23	44	60	88
Richard Sterne	263.3	137	18	37	18	122	64	142
Chris Stroud	292.3	35	16	81	15	144	59	67
Cameron Tringale	274.5	105	15	99	26	11	65	148
Yoshinobu Tsukada	269.5	125	14	115	23	44	59	67
Peter Uihlein	302.0	19	6	155	13	152	55	8
Dawie van der Walt	274.3	106	15	99	22	59	61	110
Justin Walters	285.0	57	16	81	20	92	62	123
Nick Watney	272.0	117	17	61	24	30	63	134
Bubba Watson	304.3	16	14	115	18	122	56	17
Boo Weekley	310.7	7	17	61	20	92	61	110
Lee Westwood	307.5	11	14	115	22	59	61	110
Mark Wiebe	273.3	111	15	99	20	92	66	151
Bernd Wiesberger	257.8	148	13	129	23	44	64	142
Danny Willett	304.7	14	18	37	20	92	59	67
Ashun Wu	258.0	146	12	138	17	133	59	67
YE Yang	251.0	154	18	37	20	92	63	134

Roll of Honour

Year	Champion	Score	Margin	Runners-up	Venue
1860	Willie Park Sr	174	2	Tom Morris Sr	Prestwick
1861	Tom Morris Sr	163	4	Willie Park Sr	Prestwick
1862	Tom Morris Sr	163	13	Willie Park Sr	Prestwick
1863	Willie Park Sr	168	2	Tom Morris Sr	Prestwick
1864	Tom Morris Sr	167	2	Andrew Strath	Prestwick
1865	Andrew Strath	162	2	Willie Park Sr	Prestwick
1866	Willie Park Sr	169	2	David Park	Prestwick
1867	Tom Morris Sr	170	2	Willie Park Sr	Prestwick
1868	Tommy Morris Jr	154	3	Tom Morris Sr	Prestwick
1869	Tommy Morris Jr	157	11	Bob Kirk	Prestwick
1870	Tommy Morris Jr	149	12	Bob Kirk, Davie Strath	Prestwick
1871	*No Competition*				
1872	Tommy Morris Jr	166	3	Davie Strath	Prestwick
1873	Tom Kidd	179	1	Jamie Anderson	St Andrews
1874	Mungo Park	159	2	Tommy Morris Jr	Musselburgh
1875	Willie Park Sr	166	2	Bob Martin	Prestwick
1876	Bob Martin	176	—	Davie Strath	St Andrews
	(Martin was awarded the title when Strath refused to play-off)				
1877	Jamie Anderson	160	2	Bob Pringle	Musselburgh
1878	Jamie Anderson	157	2	Bob Kirk	Prestwick
1879	Jamie Anderson	169	3	Jamie Allan, Andrew Kirkaldy	St Andrews
1880	Bob Ferguson	162	5	Peter Paxton	Musselburgh
1881	Bob Ferguson	170	3	Jamie Anderson	Prestwick
1882	Bob Ferguson	171	3	Willie Fernie	St Andrews
1883	Willie Fernie	158	Play-off	Bob Ferguson	Musselburgh
1884	Jack Simpson	160	4	Douglas Rolland, Willie Fernie	Prestwick
1885	Bob Martin	171	1	Archie Simpson	St Andrews
1886	David Brown	157	2	Willie Campbell	Musselburgh
1887	Willie Park Jr	161	1	Bob Martin	Prestwick
1888	Jack Burns	171	1	David Anderson Jr, Ben Sayers	St Andrews
1889	Willie Park Jr	155	Play-off	Andrew Kirkaldy	Musselburgh
1890	John Ball Jr*	164	3	Willie Fernie, Archie Simpson	Prestwick
1891	Hugh Kirkaldy	166	2	Willie Fernie, Andrew Kirkaldy	St Andrews
	(From 1892 the competition was extended to 72 holes)				
1892	Harold Hilton*	305	3	John Ball Jr*, Hugh Kirkaldy, Sandy Herd	Muirfield
1893	Willie Auchterlonie	322	2	John Laidlay*	Prestwick
1894	JH Taylor	326	5	Douglas Rolland	St George's
1895	JH Taylor	322	4	Sandy Herd	St Andrews
1896	Harry Vardon	316	Play-off	JH Taylor	Muirfield

Hoylake Champions: Walter Hagen (1924), Bobby Jones* (1930), Fred Daly (1947)

Year	Champion	Score	Margin	Runners-up	Venue
1897	Harold Hilton*	314	1	James Braid	Royal Liverpool
1898	Harry Vardon	307	1	Willie Park Jr	Prestwick
1899	Harry Vardon	310	5	Jack White	St George's
1900	JH Taylor	309	8	Harry Vardon	St Andrews
1901	James Braid	309	3	Harry Vardon	Muirfield
1902	Sandy Herd	307	1	Harry Vardon, James Braid	Royal Liverpool
1903	Harry Vardon	300	6	Tom Vardon	Prestwick
1904	Jack White	296	1	James Braid, JH Taylor	Royal St George's
1905	James Braid	318	5	JH Taylor, Rowland Jones	St Andrews
1906	James Braid	300	4	JH Taylor	Muirfield
1907	Arnaud Massy	312	2	JH Taylor	Royal Liverpool
1908	James Braid	291	8	Tom Ball	Prestwick
1909	JH Taylor	295	6	James Braid, Tom Ball	Cinque Ports
1910	James Braid	299	4	Sandy Herd	St Andrews
1911	Harry Vardon	303	Play-off	Arnaud Massy	Royal St George's
1912	Ted Ray	295	4	Harry Vardon	Muirfield
1913	JH Taylor	304	8	Ted Ray	Royal Liverpool
1914	Harry Vardon	306	3	JH Taylor	Prestwick
1915-1919 *No Championship*					
1920	George Duncan	303	2	Sandy Herd	Cinque Ports
1921	Jock Hutchison	296	Play-off	Roger Wethered*	St Andrews
1922	Walter Hagen	300	1	George Duncan, Jim Barnes	Royal St George's
1923	Arthur Havers	295	1	Walter Hagen	Troon
1924	Walter Hagen	301	1	Ernest Whitcombe	Royal Liverpool
1925	Jim Barnes	300	1	Archie Compston, Ted Ray	Prestwick
1926	Bobby Jones*	291	2	Al Watrous	Royal Lytham
1927	Bobby Jones*	285	6	Aubrey Boomer, Fred Robson	St Andrews
1928	Walter Hagen	292	2	Gene Sarazen	Royal St George's
1929	Walter Hagen	292	6	Johnny Farrell	Muirfield
1930	Bobby Jones*	291	2	Leo Diegel, Macdonald Smith	Royal Liverpool
1931	Tommy Armour	296	1	Jose Jurado	Carnoustie
1932	Gene Sarazen	283	5	Macdonald Smith	Prince's
1933	Denny Shute	292	Play-off	Craig Wood	St Andrews
1934	Henry Cotton	283	5	Sid Brews	Royal St George's

Year	Champion	Score	Margin	Runners-up	Venue
1935	Alf Perry	283	4	Alf Padgham	Muirfield
1936	Alf Padgham	287	1	Jimmy Adams	Royal Liverpool
1937	Henry Cotton	290	2	Reg Whitcombe	Carnoustie
1938	Reg Whitcombe	295	2	Jimmy Adams	Royal St George's
1939	Dick Burton	290	2	Johnny Bulla	St Andrews
1940-1945 *No Championship*					
1946	Sam Snead	290	4	Bobby Locke, Johnny Bulla	St Andrews
1947	Fred Daly	293	1	Reg Horne, Frank Stranahan*	Royal Liverpool
1948	Henry Cotton	284	5	Fred Daly	Muirfield
1949	Bobby Locke	283	Play-off	Harry Bradshaw	Royal St George's
1950	Bobby Locke	279	2	Roberto de Vicenzo	Troon
1951	Max Faulkner	285	2	Antonio Cerda	Royal Portrush
1952	Bobby Locke	287	1	Peter Thomson	Royal Lytham
1953	Ben Hogan	282	4	Frank Stranahan*, Dai Rees, Peter Thomson, Antonio Cerda	Carnoustie
1954	Peter Thomson	283	1	Syd Scott, Dai Rees, Bobby Locke	Royal Birkdale
1955	Peter Thomson	281	2	John Fallon	St Andrews
1956	Peter Thomson	286	3	Flory Van Donck	Royal Liverpool
1957	Bobby Locke	279	3	Peter Thomson	St Andrews
1958	Peter Thomson	278	Play-off	Dave Thomas	Royal Lytham
1959	Gary Player	284	2	Flory van Donck, Fred Bullock	Muirfield
1960	Kel Nagle	278	1	Arnold Palmer	St Andrews
1961	Arnold Palmer	284	1	Dai Rees	Royal Birkdale
1962	Arnold Palmer	276	6	Kel Nagle	Troon
1963	Bob Charles	277	Play-off	Phil Rodgers	Royal Lytham
1964	Tony Lema	279	5	Jack Nicklaus	St Andrews
1965	Peter Thomson	285	2	Christy O'Connor Sr, Brian Huggett	Royal Birkdale
1966	Jack Nicklaus	282	1	Dave Thomas, Doug Sanders	Muirfield
1967	Roberto de Vicenzo	278	2	Jack Nicklaus	Royal Liverpool
1968	Gary Player	289	2	Jack Nicklaus, Bob Charles	Carnoustie
1969	Tony Jacklin	280	2	Bob Charles	Royal Lytham
1970	Jack Nicklaus	283	Play-off	Doug Sanders	St Andrews
1971	Lee Trevino	278	1	Liang Huan Lu	Royal Birkdale
1972	Lee Trevino	278	1	Jack Nicklaus	Muirfield
1973	Tom Weiskopf	276	3	Neil Coles, Johnny Miller	Troon
1974	Gary Player	282	4	Peter Oosterhuis	Royal Lytham
1975	Tom Watson	279	Play-off	Jack Newton	Carnoustie
1976	Johnny Miller	279	6	Jack Nicklaus, Seve Ballesteros	Royal Birkdale
1977	Tom Watson	268	1	Jack Nicklaus	Turnberry
1978	Jack Nicklaus	281	2	Simon Owen, Ben Crenshaw, Ray Floyd, Tom Kite	St Andrews
1979	Seve Ballesteros	283	3	Jack Nicklaus, Ben Crenshaw	Royal Lytham
1980	Tom Watson	271	4	Lee Trevino	Muirfield
1981	Bill Rogers	276	4	Bernhard Langer	Royal St George's
1982	Tom Watson	284	1	Peter Oosterhuis, Nick Price	Royal Troon
1983	Tom Watson	275	1	Hale Irwin, Andy Bean	Royal Birkdale
1984	Seve Ballesteros	276	2	Bernhard Langer, Tom Watson	St Andrews
1985	Sandy Lyle	282	1	Payne Stewart	Royal St George's
1986	Greg Norman	280	5	Gordon J Brand	Turnberry
1987	Nick Faldo	279	1	Rodger Davis, Paul Azinger	Muirfield
1988	Seve Ballesteros	273	2	Nick Price	Royal Lytham
1989	Mark Calcavecchia	275	Play-off	Greg Norman, Wayne Grady	Royal Troon

Hoylake Champions: Alf Padgham (1936), Peter Thomson (1956), Roberto de Vicenzo (1967)

Year	Champion	Score	Margin	Runners-up	Venue
1990	Nick Faldo	270	5	Mark McNulty, Payne Stewart	St Andrews
1991	Ian Baker-Finch	272	2	Mike Harwood	Royal Birkdale
1992	Nick Faldo	272	1	John Cook	Muirfield
1993	Greg Norman	267	2	Nick Faldo	Royal St George's
1994	Nick Price	268	1	Jesper Parnevik	Turnberry
1995	John Daly	282	Play-off	Costantino Rocca	St Andrews
1996	Tom Lehman	271	2	Mark McCumber, Ernie Els	Royal Lytham
1997	Justin Leonard	272	3	Jesper Parnevik, Darren Clarke	Royal Troon
1998	Mark O'Meara	280	Play-off	Brian Watts	Royal Birkdale
1999	Paul Lawrie	290	Play-off	Justin Leonard, Jean Van de Velde	Carnoustie
2000	Tiger Woods	269	8	Ernie Els, Thomas Bjørn	St Andrews
2001	David Duval	274	3	Niclas Fasth	Royal Lytham
2002	Ernie Els	278	Play-off	Thomas Levet, Stuart Appleby, Steve Elkington	Muirfield
2003	Ben Curtis	283	1	Thomas Bjørn, Vijay Singh	Royal St George's
2004	Todd Hamilton	274	Play-off	Ernie Els	Royal Troon
2005	Tiger Woods	274	5	Colin Montgomerie	St Andrews
2006	Tiger Woods	270	2	Chris DiMarco	Royal Liverpool
2007	Padraig Harrington	277	Play-off	Sergio Garcia	Carnoustie
2008	Padraig Harrington	283	4	Ian Poulter	Royal Birkdale
2009	Stewart Cink	278	Play-off	Tom Watson	Turnberry
2010	Louis Oosthuizen	272	7	Lee Westwood	St Andrews
2011	Darren Clarke	275	3	Phil Mickelson, Dustin Johnson	Royal St George's
2012	Ernie Els	273	1	Adam Scott	Royal Lytham
2013	Phil Mickelson	281	3	Henrik Stenson	Muirfield
2014	Rory McIlroy	271	2	Sergio Garcia, Rickie Fowler	Royal Liverpool

*Denotes amateur

Records

Most Victories

6: Harry Vardon, 1896, 1898, 1899, 1903, 1911, 1914
5: James Braid, 1901, 1905, 1906, 1908, 1910; JH Taylor, 1894, 1895, 1900, 1909, 1913; Peter Thomson, 1954, 1955, 1956, 1958, 1965; Tom Watson, 1975, 1977, 1980, 1982, 1983

Most Runner-Up or Joint Runner-Up Finishes

7: Jack Nicklaus, 1964, 1967, 1968, 1972, 1976, 1977, 1979
6: JH Taylor, 1896, 1904, 1905, 1906, 1907, 1914

Oldest Winners

Tom Morris Sr, 1867, 46 years 102 days
Roberto de Vicenzo, 1967, 44 years 92 days
Harry Vardon, 1914, 44 years 41 days
Tom Morris Sr, 1864, 43 years 92 days
Phil Mickelson, 2013, 43 years 35 days
Darren Clarke, 2011, 42 years 337 days
Ernie Els, 2012, 42 years 279 days

Youngest Winners

Tommy Morris Jr, 1868, 17 years 156 days
Tommy Morris Jr, 1869, 18 years 149 days
Tommy Morris Jr, 1870, 19 years 148 days
Willie Auchterlonie, 1893, 21 years 22 days
Tommy Morris Jr, 1872, 21 years 146 days
Seve Ballesteros, 1979, 22 years 103 days

Known Oldest and Youngest Competitors

74 years, 11 months, 24 days: Tom Morris Sr, 1896
74 years, 4 months, 9 days: Gene Sarazen, 1976
14 years, 4 months, 25 days: Tommy Morris Jr, 1865

Largest Margin of Victory

13 strokes, Tom Morris Sr, 1862
12 strokes, Tommy Morris Jr, 1870
11 strokes, Tommy Morris Jr, 1869
8 strokes, JH Taylor, 1900 and 1913; James Braid, 1908; Tiger Woods, 2000

Lowest Winning Total by a Champion

267, Greg Norman, Royal St George's 1993 – 66, 68, 69, 64

268, Tom Watson, Turnberry, 1977 – 68, 70, 65, 65; Nick Price, Turnberry, 1994 – 69, 66, 67, 66
269, Tiger Woods, St Andrews, 2000 – 67, 66, 67, 69

Lowest Total in Relation to Par Since 1963

19 under par: Tiger Woods, St Andrews, 2000 (269)
18 under par: Nick Faldo, St Andrews, 1990 (270); Tiger Woods, Royal Liverpool, 2006 (270)
17 under par: Rory McIlroy, Royal Liverpool, 2014 (271)

Lowest Total by a Runner-Up

269: Jack Nicklaus, Turnberry, 1977 – 68, 70, 65, 66; Nick Faldo, Royal St George's, 1993 – 69, 63, 70, 67; Jesper Parnevik, Turnberry, 1994 – 68, 66, 68, 67

Lowest Total by an Amateur

281: Iain Pyman, Royal St George's, 1993 – 68, 72, 70, 71; Tiger Woods, Royal Lytham & St Annes, 1996 – 75, 66, 70, 70

Lowest Individual Round

63: Mark Hayes, second round, Turnberry, 1977; Isao Aoki, third round, Muirfield, 1980; Greg Norman, second round, Turnberry, 1986; Paul Broadhurst, third round, St Andrews, 1990; Jodie Mudd, fourth round, Royal Birkdale, 1991; Nick Faldo, second round, Royal St George's, 1993; Payne Stewart, fourth round, Royal St George's, 1993; Rory McIlroy, first round, St Andrews, 2010

Lowest Individual Round by an Amateur

65: Tom Lewis, first round, Royal St George's, 2011

Lowest First Round

63: Rory McIlroy, St Andrews, 2010

Lowest Second Round

63: Mark Hayes, Turnberry, 1977; Greg Norman, Turnberry, 1986; Nick Faldo, Royal St George's, 1993

Lowest Third Round

63: Isao Aoki, Muirfield, 1980; Paul Broadhurst, St Andrews, 1990

Lowest Fourth Round

63: Jodie Mudd, Royal Birkdale, 1991; Payne Stewart, Royal St George's, 1993

Lowest Score over the First 36 Holes

130: Nick Faldo, Muirfield, 1992 – 66, 64; Brandt Snedeker, Royal Lytham & St Annes, 2012 – 66, 64

Lowest Score over the Middle 36 Holes

130: Fuzzy Zoeller, Turnberry, 1994 – 66, 64

Lowest Score over the Final 36 Holes

130: Tom Watson, Turnberry, 1977 – 65, 65; Ian Baker-Finch, Royal Birkdale, 1991 – 64, 66; Anders Forsbrand, Turnberry, 1994 – 66, 64

Lowest Score over the First 54 Holes

198: Tom Lehman, Royal Lytham & St Annes, 1996 – 67, 67, 64
199: Nick Faldo, St Andrews, 1990 – 67, 65, 67; Nick Faldo, Muirfield, 1992 – 66, 64, 69; Adam Scott, Royal Lytham, 2012 – 64, 67, 68

Lowest Score over the Final 54 Holes

199: Nick Price, Turnberry, 1994 – 66, 67, 66

Lowest Score for Nine Holes

28: Denis Durnian, first nine, Royal Birkdale, 1983
29: Tom Haliburton, first nine, Royal Lytham & St Annes, 1963; Peter Thomson, first nine, Royal Lytham & St Annes, 1963; Tony Jacklin, first nine, St Andrews, 1970; Bill Longmuir, first nine, Royal Lytham & St Annes, 1979; David J Russell first nine, Royal Lytham & St Annes, 1988; Ian Baker-Finch, first nine, St Andrews, 1990; Paul Broadhurst, first nine, St Andrews, 1990; Ian Baker-Finch, first nine, Royal Birkdale, 1991; Paul McGinley, first nine, Royal Lytham & St Annes, 1996; Ernie Els, first nine, Muirfield, 2002; Sergio Garcia, first nine, Royal Liverpool, 2006

Most Successive Victories

4: Tommy Morris Jr, 1868-72 *(No Championship in 1871)*
3: Jamie Anderson, 1877-79; Bob Ferguson, 1880-82; Peter Thomson, 1954-56
2: Tom Morris Sr, 1861-62; JH Taylor, 1894-95; Harry Vardon, 1898-99; James Braid, 1905-06; Bobby Jones, 1926-27; Walter Hagen, 1928-29; Bobby Locke, 1949-50; Arnold Palmer, 1961-62; Lee Trevino, 1971-72; Tom Watson, 1982-83; Tiger Woods, 2005-06; Padraig Harrington, 2007-08

Amateurs Who Have Won The Open

3: Bobby Jones, Royal Lytham & St Annes, 1926; St Andrews, 1927; Royal Liverpool, 1930
2: Harold Hilton, Muirfield, 1892; Royal Liverpool, 1897
1: John Ball Jr, Prestwick, 1890

Champions Who Won on Debut

Willie Park Sr, Prestwick, 1860; Tom Kidd, St Andrews, 1873; Mungo Park, Musselburgh, 1874; Jock Hutchison, St Andrews, 1921; Denny Shute, St Andrews, 1933; Ben Hogan, Carnoustie, 1953; Tony Lema, St Andrews, 1964; Tom Watson, Carnoustie, 1975; Ben Curtis, Royal St George's, 2003

Greatest Interval Between First and Last Victory

19 years: JH Taylor, 1894-1913
18 years: Harry Vardon, 1896-1914
15 years: Willie Park Sr, 1860-75; Gary Player, 1959-74
14 years: Henry Cotton, 1934-48

Greatest Interval Between Victories

11 years: Henry Cotton, 1937-48 *(No Championship 1940-45)*
10 years: Ernie Els, 2002-12
9 years: Willie Park Sr, 1866-75; Bob Martin, 1876-85; JH Taylor, 1900-09; Gary Player, 1959-68

Attendance

Year	Total
1960	39,563
1961	21,708
1962	37,098
1963	24,585
1964	35,954
1965	32,927
1966	40,182
1967	29,880
1968	51,819
1969	46,001
1970	81,593
1971	70,076
1972	84,746
1973	78,810
1974	92,796
1975	85,258
1976	92,021
1977	87,615
1978	125,271
1979	134,501
1980	131,610
1981	111,987
1982	133,299
1983	142,892
1984	193,126
1985	141,619
1986	134,261
1987	139,189
1988	191,334
1989	160,639
1990	208,680
1991	189,435
1992	146,427
1993	141,000
1994	128,000
1995	180,000
1996	170,000
1997	176,000
1998	195,100
1999	157,000
2000	230,000
2001	178,000
2002	161,500
2003	183,000
2004	176,000
2005	223,000
2006	230,000
2007	154,000
2008	201,500
2009	123,000
2010	201,000
2011	180,100
2012	181,300
2013	142,036
2014	202,917

Champions Who Have Won in Three Separate Decades

Harry Vardon, 1896, 1898 & 1899/1903/1911 & 1914
JH Taylor, 1894 & 1895/1900 & 1909/1913
Gary Player, 1959, 1968, 1974

Competitors with the Most Top Five Finishes

16: JH Taylor; Jack Nicklaus

Competitors Who Have Recorded the Most Rounds Under Par From 1963

59: Jack Nicklaus
53: Nick Faldo

Competitors with the Most Finishes Under Par From 1963

14: Jack Nicklaus; Nick Faldo; Ernie Els
13: Tom Watson

Champions Who Have Led Outright After Every Round

72 hole Championships
Ted Ray, 1912; Bobby Jones, 1927; Gene Sarazen, 1932; Henry Cotton, 1934; Tom Weiskopf, 1973; Tiger Woods, 2005; Rory McIlroy, 2014
36 hole Championships
Willie Park Sr, 1860 and 1866; Tom Morris Sr, 1862 and 1864; Tommy Morris Jr, 1869 and 1870; Mungo Park, 1874; Jamie Anderson, 1879; Bob Ferguson, 1880, 1881, 1882; Willie Fernie, 1883; Jack Simpson, 1884; Hugh Kirkaldy, 1891

Largest Leads Since 1892

After 18 holes:
5 strokes: Sandy Herd, 1896
4 strokes: Harry Vardon, 1902; Jim Barnes, 1925; Christy O'Connor Jr, 1985
After 36 holes:
9 strokes: Henry Cotton, 1934
6 strokes: Abe Mitchell, 1920
After 54 holes:
10 strokes: Henry Cotton, 1934
7 strokes: Harry Vardon, 1903; Tony Lema, 1964
6 strokes: JH Taylor, 1900; James Braid, 1905; James Braid, 1908; Max Faulkner, 1951; Tom Lehman, 1996; Tiger Woods, 2000; Rory McIlroy, 2014

Champions Who Had Four Rounds, Each Better than the One Before

Jack White, Royal St George's, 1904 – 80, 75, 72, 69
James Braid, Muirfield, 1906 – 77, 76, 74, 73
Ben Hogan, Carnoustie, 1953 – 73, 71, 70, 68
Gary Player, Muirfield, 1959 – 75, 71, 70, 68

Same Number of Strokes in Each of the Four Rounds by a Champion

Denny Shute, St Andrews, 1933 – 73, 73, 73, 73 (excluding the play-off)

Best 18-Hole Recovery by a Champion

George Duncan, Deal, 1920. Duncan was 13 strokes behind the leader, Abe Mitchell, after 36 holes and level with him after 54.

Greatest Variation Between Rounds by a Champion

14 strokes: Henry Cotton, 1934, second round 65, fourth round 79
12 strokes: Henry Cotton, 1934, first round 67, fourth round 79
11 strokes: Jack White, 1904, first round 80, fourth round 69; Greg Norman, 1986, first round 74, second round 63; Greg Norman, 1986, second round 63, third round 74
10 strokes: Seve Ballesteros, 1979, second round 65, third round 75

Greatest Variation Between Two Successive Rounds by a Champion

11 strokes: Greg Norman, 1986, first round 74, second round 63; Greg Norman, 1986, second round 63, third round 74
10 strokes: Seve Ballesteros, 1979, second round 65, third round 75

Greatest Comeback by a Champion

After 18 holes
Harry Vardon, 1896, 11 strokes behind the leader
After 36 holes
George Duncan, 1920, 13 strokes behind the leader
After 54 holes
Paul Lawrie, 1999, 10 strokes behind the leader

Champions Who Had Four Rounds Under 70

Greg Norman, Royal St George's, 1993 – 66, 68, 69, 64; Nick Price, Turnberry, 1994 – 69, 66, 67, 66; Tiger Woods, St Andrews, 2000 – 67, 66, 67, 69

Competitors Who Failed to Win The Open Despite Having Four Rounds Under 70

Ernie Els, Royal St George's, 1993 – 68, 69, 69, 68; Jesper Parnevik, Turnberry, 1994 – 68, 66, 68, 67; Ernie Els, Royal Troon, 2004 – 69, 69, 68, 68; Rickie Fowler, Royal Liverpool, 2014 – 69, 69, 68, 67

Lowest Final Round by a Champion

64: Greg Norman, Royal St George's, 1993
65: Tom Watson, Turnberry, 1977; Seve Ballesteros, Royal Lytham & St Annes, 1988; Justin Leonard, Royal Troon, 1997

Worst Round by a Champion Since 1939

78: Fred Daly, third round, Royal Liverpool, 1947
76: Bobby Locke, second round, Royal St George's, 1949; Paul Lawrie, third round, Carnoustie, 1999

Champion with the Worst Finishing Round Since 1939

75: Sam Snead, St Andrews, 1946

Lowest Opening Round by a Champion

65: Louis Oosthuizen, St Andrews, 2010

Most Open Championship Appearances

46: Gary Player
39: Sandy Lyle
38: Sandy Herd, Jack Nicklaus
37: Tom Watson
36: Nick Faldo

Most Final Day Appearances Since 1892

32: Jack Nicklaus
31: Sandy Herd
30: JH Taylor
28: Ted Ray
27: Harry Vardon, James Braid, Nick Faldo
26: Peter Thomson, Gary Player, Tom Watson

Most Appearances by a Champion Before His First Victory

19: Darren Clarke, 2011; Phil Mickelson, 2013
15: Nick Price, 1994
14: Sandy Herd, 1902
13: Ted Ray, 1912; Jack White, 1904; Reg Whitcombe, 1938; Mark O'Meara, 1998

11: George Duncan, 1920; Nick Faldo, 1987; Ernie Els, 2002; Stewart Cink, 2009
10: Roberto de Vicenzo, 1967; Padraig Harrington, 2007

The Open Which Provided the Greatest Number of Rounds Under 70 Since 1946

148 rounds, Turnberry, 1994

The Open with the Fewest Rounds Under 70 Since 1946

2 rounds, St Andrews, 1946; Royal Liverpool, 1947; Carnoustie, 1968

Statistically Most Difficult Hole Since 1982

St Andrews, 1984, Par-4 17th, 4.79

Longest Course in Open History

Carnoustie, 2007, 7,421 yards

Number of Times Each Course Has Hosted The Open Championship

St Andrews, 28; Prestwick, 24; Muirfield, 16; Royal St George's, 14; Royal Liverpool, 12; Royal Lytham & St Annes, 11; Royal Birkdale, 9; Royal Troon, 8; Carnoustie, 7; Musselburgh, 6; Turnberry, 4; Royal Cinque Ports, 2; Royal Portrush and Prince's, 1

Prize Money (£)

Year	Total	First Prize	Year	Total	First Prize	Year	Total	First Prize	Year	Total	First Prize
1860	nil	nil	1889	22	8	1963	8,500	1,500	1990	825,000	85,000
1863	10	nil	1890	29.50	13	1965	10,000	1,750	1991	900,000	90,000
1864	15	6	1891	28.50	10	1966	15,000	2,100	1992	950,000	95,000
1865	20	8	1892	110	35	1968	20,000	3,000	1993	1,000,000	100,000
1866	11	6	1893	100	30	1969	30,000	4,250	1994	1,100,000	110,000
1867	16	7	1900	125	50	1970	40,000	5,250	1995	1,250,000	125,000
1868	12	6	1910	135	50	1971	45,000	5,500	1996	1,400,000	200,000
1872	unknown	8	1920	225	75	1972	50,000	5,500	1997	1,600,000	250,000
1873	unknown	11	1927	275	75	1975	75,000	7,500	1998	1,800,000	300,000
1874	20	8	1930	400	100	1977	100,000	10,000	1999	2,000,000	350,000
1876	27	10	1931	500	100	1978	125,000	12,500	2000	2,750,000	500,000
1877	20	8	1946	1,000	150	1979	155,000	15,000	2001	3,300,000	600,000
1878	unknown	8	1949	1,500	300	1980	200,000	25,000	2002	3,800,000	700,000
1879	47	10	1951	1,700	300	1982	250,000	32,000	2003	3,900,000	700,000
1880	unknown	8	1953	2,500	500	1983	310,000	40,000	2004	4,000,000	720,000
1881	21	8	1954	3,500	750	1984	451,000	55,000	2007	4,200,000	750,000
1882	47.25	12	1955	3,750	1,000	1985	530,000	65,000	2010	4,800,000	850,000
1883	20	8	1958	4,850	1,000	1986	600,000	70,000	2011	5,000,000	900,000
1884	23	8	1959	5,000	1,000	1987	650,000	75,000	2013	5,250,000	945,000
1885	35.50	10	1960	7,000	1,250	1988	700,000	80,000	2014	5,400,000	975,000
1886	20	8	1961	8,500	1,400	1989	750,000	80,000			

ROYAL LIVERPOOL

143RD OPEN CHAMPIONSHIP
Card of the Championship Course

Hole	Par	Yards	Hole	Par	Yards
1	4	458	10	5	532
2	4	454	11	4	391
3	4	426	12	4	447
4	4	372	13	3	194
5	5	528	14	4	454
6	3	201	15	3	161
7	4	480	16	5	577
8	4	431	17	4	458
9	3	197	18	5	551
Out	35	3,547	In	37	3,765
			Total	72	7,312